culloden moor 1746

the death of the jacobite cause

STUART REID

culloden moor 1746

the death of the jacobite cause

Praeger Illustrated Military History Series

PRAEGER

Westport, Connecticut
London

Library of Congress Cataloging-in-Publication Data

Reid, Stuart, 1954-
  Culloden Moor, 1746 : the death of the Jacobite cause / Stuart Reid.
    p. cm. – (Praeger illustrated military history, ISSN 1547-206X)
  Originally published: London: Osprey, 2002.
  Includes bibliographical references and index.
  ISBN 0-275-98635-7 (alk. paper)
  1. Culloden, Battle of, Scotland, 1746. 2. Jacobite Rebellion, 1745-1746. 3. Jacobites.
  I. Title. II. Series
  DA814.5.R455   2005
  941.07'2 – dc22   2004062412

British Library Cataloguing in Publication Data is available.

First published in paperback in 2003 by Osprey Publishing Limited,
Midland House, West Way, Botley, Oxford OX2 0PH, UK
443 Park Avenue South, New York, NY 10016, USA
All rights reserved.

Library of Congress Catalog Card Number: 2004062412
ISBN: 0-275-98635-7
ISSN: 1547-206X

Praeger Publishers, 88 Post Road West, Westport, CT 06881
An imprint of Greenwood Publishing Group, Inc.
www.praeger.com

Printed in China through World Print Ltd.

The paper used in this book complies with the Permanent Paper Standard issued
by the National Information Standards Organization (Z39.48-1984).

10 9 8 7 6 5 4 3 2 1

ILLUSTRATED BY: Gerry Embleton

FRONT COVER: Courtesy of the Royal Collection © 2004, Her Majesty Queen Elizabeth II

CONTENTS

KEY TO MILITARY SYMBOLS

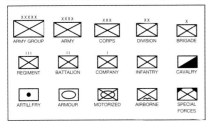

INTRODUCTION

The first steps on what would be the long road to Culloden Moor were taken in 1688 when King James II of England, and VII of Scotland, was deposed in a coup subsequently celebrated as the Glorious Revolution and the twin kingdoms of Scotland and England found themselves committed to a pan-European war against France. The war was protracted, bloody and hideously expensive, and during the course of it the two kingdoms were joined in a political Union in 1707.

This development, originally a wartime expedient aimed at better maximising the near exhausted resources of the two countries, was an unpopular one which became inextricably linked with a constitutional crisis on the death of Queen Anne in 1714.

There were two candidates for the vacant throne, and the successful one was Georg, Elector of Hanover, a great grandson of James VI of Scotland & I of England, who enjoyed the significant advantage of having served under the great Duke of Marlborough during the recent war. The other claimant was the titular King James VIII. Notwithstanding unkind stories that he was a changeling, smuggled into the Royal bedchamber in a warming-pan, there was no doubt that he was the legitimate son and heir of the late King James VII & II. While, objectively James might indeed be the 'rightful lawful King', and the Stuarts had occupied the Scottish throne since the 14th century, they had only sat on the English one for a mere 85 years and 20 of those years had been taken up with a particularly destructive civil war and interregnum. Consequently there was little or no residual affection in England for the 'Scottish' Stuarts and it is little wonder therefore that the Jacobite risings of 1715 and particularly 1745 should attract so little popular support south of the border.

Surprisingly enough support for the Stuarts north of the border was also problematic. This was because the Scots' view of kingship was very different from that held or at least outwardly professed by their southern neighbours. As long ago as the famous Declaration of Arbroath in Robert I's time it had been very firmly asserted that the King ruled only by the will of his people and that ultimate authority lay with the Estates (or parliament) as representatives of the people, and not with the man who happened to wear the crown. The Great Civil War of the 1640s had begun with the Scots repudiation of King Charles I's authority and by the end of the 17th century, just as in England, the Stuarts were unpopular with large sections of the Scottish population. Significantly, while the English Parliament rather unconvincingly represented King James VII's flight to France as an abdication, their Scottish colleagues rather more robustly declared that he had *forfaultit* the Crown and entirely legitimately offered it instead to Dutch William.

Given the very real weakness of their constitutional claim to the throne of Scotland, notwithstanding their protestations to the contrary, the only viable strategy now open to the Stuarts was to present themselves as the ancient Kings of an independent Scotland and to assume leadership of the campaign to dissolve the Union. By this means they were able to harness very considerable nationalist support, but in reality their eyes remained very firmly fixed on Whitehall and the contradictions inherent in pursuing a claim to the throne of England with an army largely made up of men dedicated to severing all links with that country became tragically apparent in 1745.

In 1715 a pro-Jacobite rising had come perilously close to success. Within Scotland opposition to the enforced Union was then at its height, while Georg of Hanover, or rather King George I, had yet to establish himself properly on the throne, and the Stuart claim to it, although shaky was at least still fresh and viable. Substantial forces were raised in James's name both in Scotland and in the north of England, but poor leadership and above all a lack of proper strategic direction eventually led to their total defeat. Some 30 years later the prospects for another uprising were considerably bleaker.

In the first place the Stuarts' constitutional claim had been well-nigh fatally weakened by the passage of time, and although there was still considerable opposition to the Union at a grassroots level, its commercial and political benefits were becoming increasingly apparent. Assessments by Jacobite agents in the late 1730s therefore gloomily concluded that if another rising was not launched soon any residual support for the Stuarts would be lost by default. Even more worryingly, most of those prepared to commit themselves to the cause bluntly stated that outside assistance was essential and that they would rise in the event of a French landing, but not otherwise.

It was unfortunate, therefore, that France displayed very little interest in landing, for her long land frontier ensured that her principal priorities lay in continental Europe. Nevertheless, in 1744 a substantial invasion force was put together in readiness for a descent on the Thames Estuary, and a smaller force earmarked for Scotland. However the primary object of the expedition was not the restoration of the Stuarts but the neutralising of British intervention in the War of the Austrian Succession. Consequently when Channel storms unexpectedly disrupted the embarkation and scattered the French battle-fleet, the attempt was abruptly abandoned and the troops marched north into Flanders instead. Behind them, impotently kicking his heels, they left Prince Charles Edward Stuart, the elder son of the would-be King James.

With his father's commission as Prince Regent in his pocket, he had hoped to go ashore with the French invasion force, but in the summer of 1745 he was offered help from a most unlikely source. Ever since the old King James had been defeated by Dutch William there had been a substantial colony of Irish exiles in Brittany, based around the ports of Nantes and St. Malo. Many of them were ship-owners and Lord Clare, the commander of the French Army's famous Irish Brigade, introduced one particular consortium to the Prince. Headed by Walter Routledge and Anthony Walsh they had originally been engaged in the slave trade between Africa and the West Indies, but this had been seriously disrupted by the war and so they had turned to privateering instead. Now, for an unspecified price, they were prepared to carry the Prince and his supporters to Scotland.

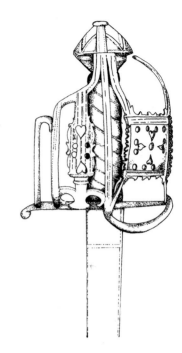

Glasgow style broadsword hilt. Most broadsword blades were in fact imported from Germany and mounted with hilts either in Stirling or Glasgow – each school having a very distinctive and easily recognised style.

On 5 July 1745 the consortium's ships cleared Belle Isle and on 23 July the Prince landed on the Hebridean island of Eriskay to an unexpectedly unfriendly welcome. Far from bringing a French Army he had just seven companions and hardly any cash or equipment. Not surprisingly the locals flatly refused to join him and instead he was rather brusquely advised to turn around and go home again. Retorting that he had come home, he moved on to the mainland and entered into a desperate round of negotiations with other potential supporters. Some measure of his difficulty in persuading them to commit themselves is the fact that the rebel standard was not raised until nearly a month later, at Glenfinnan on 19 August. By that time, the Government was only too well aware of what was going on and the Commander-in-Chief, North Britain had been ordered into the Highlands.

With the European war then at its height the forces available to Lieutenant-General Sir John Cope were far from prepossessing either in numbers or in quality. Even on paper he could muster little more than $3\frac{1}{2}$ battalions of infantry and two regiments of cavalry. However, one of those battalions, Guise's 6th Foot, was garrisoning the various Highland forts and two companies of another, Lascelles 58th Foot, were in Edinburgh Castle. It was also considered impractical to take the cavalry into the hills and in the end Cope assembled only the ten companies of Murray's 57th Foot, eight companies of Lascelles' 58th, five companies of Lee's 55th Foot and two Additional (or depot) companies of recruits for the 43rd Highlanders.

Marching from Stirling on 20 August he hoped to augment this little force with loyalist volunteers, but all he actually succeeded in picking up en route was an incomplete company of recruits for Loudoun's 64th Highlanders. Nevertheless, notwithstanding this apparent apathy

Ruthven Barracks, as viewed from the point where Gordon of Glenbuchat emplaced his guns during the second (successful) siege of the barracks in February 1746. The photograph clearly illustrates how the barracks were constructed in a strong position on the motte of the old Ruthven Castle.

PRESTONPANS (pages 10–11)

The last Jacobite Rising is often portrayed in terms of a clash between the emerging modern British state and the last doomed remnants of an ancient tribal society. To some extent this picture is overdrawn in that there was and always had been a close relationship between Highland and Lowland Scots society and by the middle of the 18th century the processes of social change, commercial development and overpopulation which would eventually lead to the Highland Clearances was well underway. In central Scotland the Industrial Revolution had already begun. Not only was the area pock-marked by coal-pits and embryonic slag heaps, but the first waggonways or railways were being laid to carry the coal down to the waiting cargo ships and iron foundries. These early waggonways still had for the most part wooden rails and the wagons that used them were individually drawn by horses, but yet they were unmistakably railways – and one of them ran straight across Cope's battlefield at Prestonpans. It was not raised up on an embankment and so had no military significance, but as the Highland Army tried to manoeuvre around him Cope redeployed his army several times. At last in the early hours of the morning it became clear that the Jacobites would attack from the east and so Cope drew up his army for the last time in the dark, aligning it along the railway track that conveniently ran from north to south (1).

The Jacobites' intention had simply been to launch an unsophisticated frontal assault on Cope's infantry, but due to a combination of darkness, fog, inexperience and poor staff work they quite accidentally avoided the infantry entirely and routed the dragoons posted on either flank. They thus escaped the heavy casualties that might otherwise have been inflicted by the infantry's volley-fire. Instead, while most of the clansmen following the Camerons' red and yellow striped banner (2) exuberantly chased after the fugitive dragoons, others turned on the exposed flank of Cope's infantry (3) and rolled it up in very short order. The end result was that not only did the rebels win a dramatic and decisive victory at very little cost, but both sides also gained an exaggerated impression of the effectiveness of a Highland Charge.

Nevertheless there is an appropriate irony in the fact that the Highlanders' only major victory in the campaign should take place not amongst their own heather covered hills and glens, but on a flat and peaceful stubble-covered cornfield, set in a semi-industrialised landscape and it is likely that while only a handful of Jacobites were killed, one or two of the victorious clansmen may just possibly have injured at least their pride tripping over a very unfamiliar obstacle (4). **(Gerry Embleton)**

The rear gate at Ruthven Barracks. In 1745 a party of rebel sappers tried to burn through it with a barrel of combustibles, but were shot down from the loopholes in the flanking tower and the barrel then extinguished by water poured over the wall.

Cope did at least have access to a very efficient intelligence network and at Dalwhinnie he received definite information that the rebels planned to fight him in the steep traverses of the Corryairack Pass. Judging the position too strong to be forced Cope abandoned his original intention of establishing a forward base at Fort Augustus, and recognising the political consequences of retreating, instead marched north to Inverness.

Disappointed in their expectation that the General would obligingly march into the trap prepared for him, the rebels were initially thrown off balance by this move. Their immediate reaction was to follow Cope to Inverness, but eventually the temptation of marching directly on Edinburgh proved too much. Masking the move with an unsuccessful assault on Ruthven Barracks on 29 August – it was held by just 12 men under Sergeant Terry Molloy – they moved south and took Perth on 3 September. After resting up for a week they set off again, crossed the Forth on 13 September, and then in rather mysterious circumstances seized Edinburgh on the night of 17/18 September.

Ironically, having reached Inverness Cope was at last joined by some useful reinforcements. He had already taken a company of Guise's 6th Foot from Ruthven, now he found another in Inverness, with three incomplete companies of the 64th Highlanders and a 200-strong loyalist battalion raised by Captain George Monro of Culcairn. Only too aware of the danger to the capital, he marched hard for Aberdeen, embarked his forces on ships there and arrived off Dunbar on 17 September. He was just 24 hours too late to save Edinburgh, but still determined to retrieve the situation, he nevertheless marched westwards and finding the rebels also spoiling for a fight he halted on a flat cornfield outside Prestonpans on 20 September.

From Cope's point of view he was in an ideal position with clear fields of fire for his infantry and artillery, and no impediments to hinder a charge by the two regiments of dragoons that had rejoined him at Dunbar. In theory he had everything going for him but ironically, it was a blunder on the part of the rebel commanders that was to inadvertently cost him the battle.

For their part the Jacobites had taken up what appeared to be their own ideal position on Falside Hill, to the south, from where they could charge down on Cope's army. When taking a closer look however the rebel commanders discovered to their chagrin that a bog lay at the foot of the hill which would effectively stop any charge in its tracks. After some to-ing and fro-ing, recrimination and discussion they eventually decided to swing around to their right under cover of darkness and attack Cope from the east. The move got off to an inauspicious start when barking dogs alerted the general to the fact that something was happening and when the rebels crossed the bog by a supposedly little-known track they found it covered by a picquet of dragoons. This particular misfortune may be attributed to the fact that the dragoons' commander, Colonel James Gardiner, was not only a local man but actually owned the land in question and was therefore well aware of the existence of the path.

Cope and his men were therefore soon alerted to both the imminence and the direction of the rebel assault, and far from being caught asleep as the popular song suggests, were ready and waiting for them, deployed behind a colliery railway track or waggonway crossing an 'extensive corn field, plain and level, without a bush or tree'. On the left were Hamilton's 14th Dragoons, then Murray's 57th Foot, Lascelles' 58th (including the two companies of Guise's 6th) and the half battalion of Lee's 55th. On the right wing were six light curricle guns and four small Coehorn mortars, with an artillery guard drawn from the infantry battalions, and finally Gardiner's 13th Dragoons.

They did not have long to wait in this position and a loyalist volunteer, John Home, recalled that: 'Harvest was just got in, and the ground was covered with a thick stubble, which rustled under the feet of the Highlanders as they ran on, speaking and muttering in a manner that expressed and heightened their fierceness and rage. When they set out the mist was very thick; but before they had got half-way, the sun rose, dispelled the mist, and showed the armies to each other.'

What it also showed was that in contrast to Cope's men the rebels had made a complete cock of their deployment. They had divided themselves in two wings, the right comprising three battalions of MacDonalds under the Duke of Perth, and the left comprising the Camerons, Stewarts of Appin and Perth's regiment under Lord George Murray. In the hurry to deploy in the mist they had become widely separated so when they went forward they each attacked the outer flanks of Cope's army. Thoroughly intimidated by the sheer weight of numbers thrown against them, the dragoons and artillerymen fled leaving the infantry with no enemy to their front and their flanks wide open. Consequently the Highlanders then simply rolled up the infantry line and as Major John Severn of Lascelles' afterwards testified: 'A large Body of their Left rush'd on obliquely on our Right Flank, and broke the Foot as it were by Platoons, with so rapid a Motion, that the whole Line was broken in a few Minutes.'

In those few minutes the British Army lost some 150 dead and 1,326 prisoners, while the Rebels on the other hand admitted to five officers and 30 men killed and another 70–80 wounded. It was by any accounting a famous victory, but it was far from decisive.

CHRONOLOGY

1745

5 July Jacobite expedition clears Belle Isle, France

9 July Expedition unsuccessfully intercepted by HMS *Lion*

25 July Prince Charles Edward lands at Loch nan Uamh

16 August Two Additional (depot) Coys. 1st (Royal) Regt. captured at Invergarry

19 August Rebel standard raised at Glenfinnan

20 August Sir John Cope marches north from Stirling

26 August Cope avoids contact with the rebels and marches for Inverness

29 August Unsuccessful rebel assault on Ruthven Barracks

3 September Rebels capture Perth

17 September Rebels capture Edinburgh
Cope's men arrive by ship off Dunbar

21 September *Battle of Prestonpans*

31 October Rebels march for England

1 November Field Marshal Wade completes concentration of army at Newcastle

15 November Carlisle surrenders to rebels after short siege

29 November Rebels take Manchester

6 December Rebels turn back at Derby

18 December Rearguard action at Clifton

20 December Rebels re-cross border into Scotland

23 December Rebel victory over loyalist troops at Inverurie outside Aberdeen

30 December Rebel garrison of Carlisle surrenders

1746

8 January Rebels capture Stirling and lay siege to castle

17 January *Battle of Falkirk*

1 February Rebels evacuate Stirling and retire northwards

6 February British Army occupies Perth

11 February Ruthven Barracks surrendered

18 February Rebels capture Inverness

27 February British Army goes into winter quarters at Aberdeen

5 March Rebels capture Fort Augustus

20 March Earl of Loudoun's loyalist army dispersed at Dornoch
Successful rebel raid on Keith

12 April British Army crosses river Spey

15 April Rebels launch abortive night attack on Nairn

16 April *Battle of Culloden*

OPPOSING COMMANDERS

JACOBITE COMMANDERS

Prince Charles Edward Stuart (1720–1788) Born in Bologna the 'Young Italian' came to Scotland with little more than his father's commission to act as Prince Regent and a determination that bordered on obsession to regain the twin thrones of Scotland and England. On the positive side he was young, extremely fit, handsome and charismatic. In physical terms, there is no doubt that he was in ideal shape to act as the dashing leader of an insurrection. At a more practical level, however, his enthusiasm for military operations was not matched by his technical expertise and his otherwise commendable determination ultimately blinded him to the practical difficulties of achieving his objectives. Unfortunately this in turn led to a certain degree of instability and a tendency to abdicate all responsibility for the management of his army in times of crisis. Consequently he was extremely fortunate to have a competent chief of staff. In all three of the major battles his presence was decorative rather than useful and afterwards he fled into an alcoholic exile.

Colonel John William Sullivan (b.1700) Born in County Kerry, Colonel Sullivan had entered the French Army in 1721 and served under *Marechal* Maillebois in Corsica, Italy and on the Rhine, gaining considerable experience of irregular warfare. By 1745 he was a captain on the General Staff and on the strength of his experience he was offered a colonel's commission and appointed Prince Charles' chief-of-staff as both Adjutant-General and Quartermaster-General of the Jacobite Army. Unfortunately he and the most forceful of the rebel lieutenant-generals, Lord George Murray, took an instant dislike to each other and as the latter's version of events was published a century before Sullivan's, the stoutly built Irishman has come to be cast as an incompetent buffoon who exercised a malign and ultimately fatal influence over the Prince. In reality he was a very capable and professional staff officer, and at Culloden was effectively left in sole charge of the army. Afterwards he returned to the French Army and served on the staff at Lauffelt in 1747. Although close to the Prince during the rising the two became estranged after Sullivan ran off with his mistress!

Lord George Murray (1694–1760) was a brother of the Duke of Atholl, and his background excited suspicion from the outset. In 1715 he had thrown up a regular commission as an ensign in the Royal Scots to join the Jacobites. He also fought at Glenshiel in 1719 but was pardoned in 1726 and in 1745 tried without success to raise loyalist volunteers for Sir John Cope's army. His defection to the rebels came rather late in the day and although he was at once appointed a lieutenant-general in recognition of

Prince Charles Edward Stuart, an early portrait after Domenica Dupre. While the warlike attitude was a conventional one in an age when princes were still expected to lead armies, the Young Chevalier displayed a genuine if erratic interest in military matters.

RIGHT **James Drummond, Duke of Perth (1713–1746), as depicted by McIan, but based on a contemporary portrait. Although appointed a lieutenant-general he was generally overshadowed by the domineering Lord George Murray. Escaping from Culloden he died on board the ship carrying him to France, and his title passed to his younger brother Lord John Drummond.**

his supposed local influence, many of his colleagues regarded him with considerable suspicion and long after the Rising there was a popular tradition that he was a traitor. One of his ADCs, James Johnstone described him as 'vigilant, active and diligent; his plans were always judiciously formed, and he carried them promptly and vigorously into execution. However, with an infinity of good qualities, he was not without his defects: proud, haughty, blunt and imperious, he wished to have the exclusive disposal of everything and, feeling his superiority, would listen to no advice.' Not without foundation Sullivan regarded him as an over-enthusiastic amateur, and his ill-conceived night attack on the British Army's cantonments around Nairn on the night of 15 April certainly ended in near disaster. At Culloden however he fought bravely as a brigade commander and afterwards escaped into exile in Holland.

James Drummond, Duke of Perth. Once memorably dismissed as a 'silly horse-raising boy', Perth was personally very popular and not without some ability. Appointed a lieutenant-general at the outset he stood down while the army was in England, partly in order to avoid the bad publicity that would be generated by an overtly catholic commander, and partly as a sop to the temperamental Lord George Murray. Although he again took up his appointment on returning to Scotland, Murray had by then attained a moral superiority and Perth was thereafter little more than a brigade commander. Escaping from Culloden he died at sea on the way into exile in France.

Lord John Drummond. The younger brother of the Duke of Perth he was originally an officer in the Irish Regiment Dillon, but raised his own *Royal Ecossois* in August 1744. Appointed a Brigadier he commanded all the French troops sent to Scotland and at Culloden was notionally in command of the centre 'division' in the front line. In actual fact he spent most of the battle with his brother on the left. A sometimes careless and far from enterprising officer he succeeded his brother as Duke of Perth but died at the siege of Bergen op Zoom in 1747.

John Roy Stuart. One of the Jacobite Army's few professional soldiers, he originally served in the 2nd Dragoons (Scots Greys) before going into the French service as a captain of the grenadier company of the *Royal Ecossois*. In 1745 he returned to Scotland and raised a regiment for the Prince, but normally served as a staff officer. At Culloden he

commanded the reserve. A noted adventurer he was the original inspiration for Robert Louis Stevenson's character Allan Breck Stuart – the real one being a rather unprepossessing character.

BRITISH COMMANDERS

William Augustus, Duke of Cumberland (1721–1765). The second and favourite son of King George II his military career was accelerated accordingly and by 1745 he was colonel of the 1st Footguards and captain-general of British forces at home and abroad. Nevertheless, his father had brought him up to be a conscientious soldier and throughout his career he relied very heavily on the advice and support of an 'Old Army' mafia of professional soldiers. The result was that he turned into an excellent administrator and a solid if uninspired commander. Essentially cautious his operations during the campaign were consequently characterised by careful and methodical preparation – and a lack of mistakes.

Henry Hawley (1679–1759) Commander-in-Chief, North Britain, and an important member of the army's professional mafia Hawley's first commission dated from 1694. A captain of dragoons by 1706 he became lieutenant-colonel in 1712, was a major-general in 1739, colonel of the 1st (Royal) Dragoons in 1740 and a lieutenant-general in 1743. He is all too often characterised as a brutal martinet of limited ability and James Wolfe, who had served as one of his ADCs at Culloden, wrote in 1755 that 'The troops dread his severity, hate the man, and hold his military knowledge in contempt'. Wolfe's opinion however was coloured by what he regarded as Hawley's culpable failure to complete the destruction of the rebel army at Culloden by cutting off their retreat. In reality Hawley was in fact a capable officer and military theorist, but he was in his late 60s by 1746 and essentially cautious. It may also be worth remarking that there is little real evidence of his 'severity'. Although possessed of a sergeant-major's colourful turn of phrase, his bark was normally worse than his bite and his brutal reputation largely rests on an undoubtedly black but very real sense of humour.

Humphrey Bland (1686–1763) A major-general commanding a regular cavalry brigade at Culloden, Bland's first commission dated back to 1704. He was the British Army's foremost military theoretician and his *Treatise of Military Discipline*, first published in 1727 and appearing in nine subsequent editions, formed the basis of the official 1728 *Regulations* still in force in 1746.

John Huske (1692–1761) A competent and very conscientious officer, he was universally known by his men as 'Daddy' Huske. A major-general he served as Hawley's second in command at Falkirk in January 1746 and then as commander of the second line at Culloden he ordered the decisive counter-

William Augustus, Duke of Cumberland (1721–1765), at Culloden, by David Morier. Scarlet coat with dark blue facings and gold lace. Saddle housings are also red and gold. The regiment in the background, which can be identified as Pulteney's 13th Foot. has black gaiters. (National Museums of Scotland)

attack which defeated the rebel assault on the left wing and so decided the battle.

Hugh Abercromby, Lord Sempill. First serving as an ensign under Marlborough at Malplaquet in 1709, he was successively colonel of the 43rd Highlanders (Black Watch) in 1741 and the 25th (Edinburgh) Regiment in 1745. Promoted to brigadier-general in that year his precise role at Culloden is unclear. While he was certainly a brigade commander some sources suggest he commanded the left of the front line, i.e. the 3rd Brigade but in actual fact he appears to have commanded the 4th Brigade, standing in the second line, and as such led the decisive counter-attack ordered by Major-General Huske. After Culloden he was appointed governor of Aberdeen and died there in November 1746.

Sir John Cope. Although not at Culloden, his status as commander of the British forces at Prestonpans merits a few words. Entering the army as a cornet in the 1st Dragoons in 1707, he was a major-general by 1739, a lieutenant-general in 1743 and appointed Commander-in-Chief, North Britain, in 1745. Described as a 'neat fussy little man' he owed his appointment to his social connections rather than any outstanding merit. He appears to have been a competent enough officer, but unenterprising and too obsessed with detail to see the bigger picture, with the result that although his personal bravery is unquestioned he was a rather timid commander.

ANALYSIS

Notwithstanding individual shortcomings command and control of the British Army during this campaign was straightforward since units were permanently grouped into brigades under nominated commanders. All of the officers involved were professional soldiers and staff work was generally efficient, particularly during the final advance to contact at Culloden. The only real weakness was an apparent widespread reluctance to employ cavalry aggressively in a reconnaissance role and to rely instead on a (surprisingly effective) intelligence network.

The command structure of the Jacobite Army by contrast was a complete shambles. Most major strategic decisions were taken by a council of war, while tactical ones were taken in a frighteningly haphazard fashion. In theory the Prince acted as commander-in-chief, but delegated the executive function to his chief-of-staff, Colonel Sullivan. The army's front line was arbitrarily divided into three 'divisions' (actually brigades) commanded by Lord George Murray, Lord John Drummond and the Duke of Perth respectively. Largely through force of personality Murray normally commanded the right wing, while Perth had the left, but the common convention of regarding the right of the line as the post of honour led to the absurd practice of rotating units through it in turn with the result that unlike regular brigades the composition of the Jacobite ones could change from day to day. At the best of times this was inefficient in management terms, and exacerbated by personality clashes between Lord George Murray and a number of regimental commanders – especially the MacDonalds – and particularly between Murray and Sullivan. Unsurprisingly this led to very poor co-ordination at a tactical level.

OPPOSING ARMIES

THE JACOBITE ARMY

The rebel army liked to call itself the 'Highland' Army and it is not difficult to understand why. At the most obvious level instructions such as those issued by Lord Lewis Gordon that all his men 'are to be well cloathed, with short cloathes, plaid, new shoes and three pair of hose and accoutered with shoulder ball gun, pistolls and sword' ensured that the army had a readily identifiable uniform. Although some difficulties were encountered in finding sufficient tartan jackets, plaids and hose for all of the Lowland recruits, this was a much more practical expedient than trying to have more conventional uniforms made up. Rather more importantly however it also enabled the Jacobites to capitalise on their best military asset: the fearsome reputation of the Highland clansman.

By laying stress on the claim that they were a Highland Army they not only boosted their own morale by asserting that they were all members of a military elite, rather than just a very ordinary collection of half-trained insurgents – they also hoped with some success to convince their opponents of the same thing.

In reality the army which assembled at Edinburgh after Prestonpans comprised both a Highland Division and a Lowland Division. The first was made up of the clan regiments from the Western Highlands which had fought at Prestonpans, while the latter, perhaps a little surprisingly, included units such as the Atholl Brigade which had some claim to being Highlanders but were considered steadier and a lot less 'wild' than the MacDonalds and Camerons in the first.

Otherwise the organisation of the army left something to be desired. Essentially commissions to raise regiments and companies were issued rather optimistically. A number of clan chiefs such as Cameron of Locheil were capable of levying large regiments, while others such as the Laird of MacLachlan could muster only a handful of followers. Similarly some lowland gentlemen such as Lord Ogilvie and the Duke of Perth were able to raise respectable sized units, while others were much less successful. Thus, in Aberdeenshire, James Crichton of Auchengoul obtained a colonel's commission but never seems to have recruited more than about 30 men, and probably a good deal fewer. In the early days these small regiments with far too many officers led to all manner of organisational problems, and Sullivan grumbled that: 'All was confused… such a chiefe of a tribe had sixty men, another thirty, another twenty, more or lesse; they would not mix nor seperat, & wou'd have double officers, yt is two Captns & two Lts, to each Compagny, strong or weak… but by little & little, were brought into a certain regulation.' This was done by disbanding or amalgamating the smaller

British grenadier in marching order after an unknown artist from the Penicuik area who compiled an astonishing portfolio of sketches of British regulars, Loyalist Volunteers and Militia, and Jacobite soldiers passing through Edinburgh during the campaign.

units, or simply absorbing them into larger ones. Crichton's men for example were probably incorporated in the regiment of footguards raised for Lord Kilmarnock in Aberdeenshire by his formidable mother-in-law, Lady Erroll.

It should also be pointed out that a fair degree of compulsion was used in raising those men. There were some genuine volunteers of course but the greater number of the men in the ranks joined up because their landlord or clan chief told them to, and sometimes the summons had to be accompanied by threats and even violence. Others were effectively mercenaries hired to fill the quotas demanded from Lowland districts by officers such as Lord Lewis Gordon and obviously in both cases their lack of commitment to the Jacobite cause contributed to the army's high rate of desertion.

At Prestonpans the Jacobite army's equipment had also left much to be desired. An admittedly hostile eyewitness, Patrick Crichton of Woodhouselee described how they were armed with a wide selection of firearms, many of them fowling pieces and 'some tyed with puck threed [string] to the stock, some withowt locks and some matchlocks'. Others only had swords or Lochaber Axes, and there were also the obligatory pitchforks and scythes. Effectively in fact it was only the officers and the 'gentlemen' in the front rank who were armed with the combination of broadsword, targe and pistol popularly associated with clansmen.

Afterwards however the Jacobites not only increased their numbers, but also improved their equipment. Initially both John Gordon of Glenbuchat's Regiment and the first battalion of Lord Ogilvy's were wholly armed with Land Pattern firelocks and bayonets taken from Cope's army, while other units received French ones. Some 1,500 to 1,600 stand of arms were landed at Montrose by blockade runners in October alone (probably of the Model 1717) and other shipments followed, including some Spanish weapons landed at Peterhead. The result was that by the time Culloden was fought the whole army was properly equipped with .69 cal. French or Spanish military firelocks.

Indeed it is very noticeable that while the named highland gentlemen caricatured by a contemporary artist in Edinburgh do indeed brandish broadsword and targe, by far the greater number of the ordinary Jacobite soldiers even at that early stage were armed not with broadswords but with firelock and bayonet. This visual evidence is also confirmed by the fact that in the aftermath of Culloden Cumberland reported that his clearance squads had recovered 2,320 firelocks from the battlefield but only 192 broadswords!

Nevertheless the broadsword remained the most potent symbol of the Highland soldier for it lay at the heart of a rough and ready but frighteningly effective tactical system. In short, instead of trying to win the firefight before closing with the enemy, they attempted – with considerable success at Prestonpans – to rely instead on speed and sheer intimidation by attacking immediately. Nevertheless they remained alive to the inherent weaknesses of this approach and in a perceptive memorandum compiled after the Falkirk fiasco in January 1746: '...the best of the Highland officers, whilst they remained at Falkirk after the battle, were absolutely convinced that, except they could attack the enemy at a very considerable advantage, either by surprise or by some

Clansman with a curved sword or *turcael* after the Penicuik artist. Judging by the frequency with which they appear in the sketchbook, these weapons were very popular although few survive.

strong situation of ground, or a narrow pass, they could not expect any great success, especially if their numbers were no ways equal, and that a body of regular troops was absolutely necessary to support them, when they should at any time go in, sword in hand; for they were sensible, that without more leisure and time to discipline their own men, it would not be possible to make them keep their ranks, or rally soon enough upon any sudden emergency, so that any small number of the enemy, either keeping in a body when they were in confusion, or rallying, would deprive them of a victory, even after they had done their best.'

In theory the Lowland Division, being both more regularly equipped and more amenable to training and discipline, should have carried out this supporting role, but rather too many of them simply ran away at Falkirk. At Culloden some of them would perforce have to reinforce the clansmen in the front line while the others would be almost wholly taken up with fending off an unexpected threat which developed in the rear. In the end the only support available to the front line would be two small battalions of French regulars and a newly raised Lowland one (Lord Kilmarnock's) which had only been issued with firelocks a few days before the battle.

There is no doubt that in conventional terms the Jacobite artillery and cavalry were the least effective arms. While it is quite untrue that the artillery's performance at Culloden was hampered by a multiplicity of calibres – all but one of those actually emplaced on the moor were 3-pdrs, and the exception was brought up after the engagement began by a French engineer officer named Du Saussey – it is certainly true that dragging it around proved to be more trouble than it was worth since the army's tactical doctrine relied on speed rather than firepower.

On the other hand the cavalry was actually quite useful. Although an English volunteer named John Daniel acknowledged his dismay at Falkirk when 'We were about four hundred light Horse ordered to face the enemy's dragoons…' the prospect of their doing so was quite exceptional. Ordinarily they were employed not as battle cavalry but as light horse in the reconnaissance role, at which some, particularly Bagot's Hussars, grew very proficient.

THE FRENCH

In the later stages of the campaign the Jacobites were joined by various contingents of French regulars, commanded by Lord John Drummond, a younger brother of the Duke of Perth. In addition to technical specialists such as artillerymen and engineers, there were eventually two infantry battalions and a squadron of cavalry, all drawn from the famous Irish Brigade. One of the infantry battalions was a composite formation initially made up from picquets drawn from three different Irish regiments: Dillon, Lally and Rooth, although it was later joined by a picquet from the Regiment Berwick as well. (A second picquet of Berwick was captured after landing in the far north of Scotland.) The other battalion represented the greater part of Drummond's own newly raised regiment, the *Royal Ecossois*. It was also intended to ship over the whole of the cavalry regiment *Fitzjames Cavallerie* or Fitzjames's Horse, but most of it was captured en route and only the equivalent of a single squadron was actually landed at Aberdeen.

Highland gentleman by McIan; this particular painting provides a good illustration of a Jacobite officer, perhaps a company commander, dressed in a more fashionable style than the older officer on page 6. Note the extent to which the upper garments, coat and waistcoat, tend to obscure the kilt.

OPPOSITE TOP **Lochaber axe; a desperate shortage of firearms in 1715 saw this weapon turned out in large numbers by Aberdeen blacksmiths, but it was still used in 1745 as a substitute for the more expensive broadsword.**

A very high proportion of the mercenaries serving in the ranks of all these units were deserters and 'turned' prisoners of war and in fact the majority of the troopers in Fitzjames's Horse were English, not Irish, and actually included a fair number of merchant seamen. Nearly half of the Irish Picquets who actually fought at Culloden had been press-ganged from the ranks of the prisoners of Guise's 6th Foot taken at Fort Augustus shortly before. There were also a few deserters serving in the *Royal Ecossois*, and Drummond also tried to enlist men for a second battalion after arriving in Scotland.

French tactical doctrines fitted in well with Jacobite ones, especially as some French officers helped train the Lowland units. Essentially they boiled down to manoeuvring in column, fighting in a four-rank-deep line and relying upon shock action with the bayonet rather than firepower. If it did come down to a firefight the usual practice was to commence with firing by ranks and then continue with a *feu a billebaude*, which essentially meant every soldier loading and firing in his own time.

THE BRITISH ARMY

The popular view of the British Army at Culloden is still coloured by contemporary propaganda and the stilted imagery of the 1742 *Cloathing Book*, but some remarkable eyewitness sketches by an artist from Penicuik reveal soldiers who apart from their swords would probably not have looked out of place in the Falklands 250 years later, an initial impression which is amply confirmed by study of surviving records, diaries and letters.

The infantry was the most important element, organised in battalions which in the field rarely exceeded 400 bayonets and often averaged little more than 300 apiece. Their clothing and equipment is often contrasted unfavourably with that of their rebel opponents and claimed to be tight and cumbersome, but in fact it was both practical and comfortable; comprising a red double-breasted greatcoat, canvas gaiters to protect the legs from mud (and heather) and a broad-brimmed slouch hat, a firelock and bayonet, a sword (if it had not been 'lost') and the usual impedimenta of knapsack, haversack and canteen required by all soldiers, rebel or regular.

Ordinarily the basic tactical philosophy boiled down to moving into fairly close proximity to the enemy, halting and then blazing away until fire superiority was achieved and the opposing unit retired or even ran away. The conventional view, with a fairly solid history of success in Marlborough's war to back it up, was that winning the firefight depended on being able to maintain a steady rolling fire and the chosen method of delivering that was Platooning as codified by Humphrey Bland in his immensely influential *Treatise of Military Discipline* and enshrined in the 1728 *Regulations*. This required a battalion to be divided into a series of ad hoc platoons each of between 20–30 men who would then fire in a pre-arranged sequence rippling up and down the line. Despite its limitations Platooning was effective enough in conventional operations, especially against the French whose fire discipline was notoriously bad, but service against the Highlanders revealed a fatal flaw. The deliberately paced rate of fire, while well adapted to maintaining a sustained firefight,

ABOVE **Highland sentry after the Penicuick artist. This unusually careful sketch provides one of the best contemporary illustrations of a typical Jacobite soldier, wearing highland clothes but equipped with a firelock and bayonet rather than the archaic sword and targe. Normally the plaid was pinned on the left shoulder, but as here could just as easily be wrapped around the upper body for warmth or protection from rain.**

Fine study of a highland sentry after the Penicuick artist, again with his plaid wrapped around his upper body for warmth. In addition to his firelock and bayonet this man also has a sword, probably one of the cheap broadswords brought from France, or even scavenged from Cope's battlefield.

simply could not kill enough clansmen quickly enough to stop a determined, fast-moving Highland charge.

Consequently a change of tactics was clearly called for and at Culloden heavy massed battalion volleys would be employed with excellent results. There was of course an obvious danger that having fired off everything at once the battalion might then be caught helplessly reloading if the Highlanders ignored their casualties and pressed home the attack. This danger however was obviated by the remarkable expedient, pioneered by some units at Falkirk, of directing the front rank not to reload after that first volley, but instead to charge their bayonets as soon as they had fired, thus protecting the second and third ranks as they reloaded and poured in a succession of volleys at point blank range.

Unfortunately the cavalry displayed no such tactical virtuosity. The Dragoons who made up the bulk of the cavalry regiments employed against the Jacobites had originally been mounted infantry and fought (perhaps for the last time) in this role at Clifton in December 1745, but ordinarily they were employed almost exclusively as heavy battle cavalry. Consequently although the British Army enjoyed an overwhelming numerical superiority in the mounted arm its commanders consistently failed to exploit that superiority in the all-important scouting and intelligence gathering role – an omission which is all the more remarkable in that most of them had a cavalry background. Only Kingston's provincial regiment was employed as light horse and they, for all their later reputation, were usually outclassed as scouts by their rebel counterparts.

There was no doubting on the other hand the superiority of the Royal Artillery at Culloden, although in all fairness it should be noted that its effectiveness has been overstated. The guns were a mixture of light 3-pdrs and Coehorn mortars and the stories, which are still circulated, that the Jacobites were subjected to accurate artillery fire for upwards of half an hour before commencing their attack are grossly exaggerated.

In addition to these regular forces the army was able to call upon the assistance of a substantial body of Loyalist volunteers and some other, less enthusiastic levies. The famous Argyll Militia was undoubtedly the most prominent of all the Loyalist formations, but active opposition to the 'Jacks' in the Highlands was by no means confined to Clan Campbell. During most of the rebellion Inverness was held for the Crown by a Loyalist army substantially made up of Independent Companies recruited in the northern and western Highlands – and including a fair number of Skye Macdonalds. In combat they generally proved to be as brittle as might be expected of ill-trained and poorly motivated levies, but when stiffened with regulars and properly led, as the Argylls were at Culloden, they could be quite effective.

The same, obviously, was true of the various provincial regiments raised in England, some of whom participated in the recapture of Carlisle, and the Lowlands. The most important of these was the Earl of Home's Brigade comprised of Scottish provincial regiments which successfully defended the Forth crossings late in 1745 and afterwards fought at Falkirk. Even the various rag-tag local volunteer militias such as the Derby Blues or the Aberdeen Militia were of some use in that they could be employed on rudimentary constabulary duties which would otherwise have had to be performed by regulars, and just as importantly

RIGHT **Corporal Jones of Pulteney's 13th Foot after a sketch by that regiment's Captain Baillie. Although drawn in 1753 neither the uniform nor the drill would have altered very much since 1746. Note the large amount of room required to load the firelock which in turn meant that the ranks and files were much more open than they would become in later years.**

FAR RIGHT **'Push your Bayonet' as demonstrated by a grenadier of Pulteney's 13th Foot. This particular technique proved effective enough on the defensive, as at Falkirk and Culloden, but within a few years James Wolfe would introduce the Prussian practice of levelling the bayonet at the hip instead, thus allowing it to be used offensively.**

by their very existence they deterred spontaneous tumults and even uprisings.

Of rather more dubious utility however were the wretched Vestry Men drafted into the ranks of regular regiments. Unlike their rebel counterparts most of King George's soldiers were volunteers, but at the height of the emergency in 1745 two acts were rushed through Parliament encouraging magistrates to press-gang 'all able-bodied men who do not follow or exercise any lawful calling or employment'. For each reluctant recruit thus delivered over to the army £3.00 sterling was paid into their parish Vestry account for the upkeep of any dependants left behind. Popular prejudice notwithstanding the army was actually fairly particular about where it found its recruits and viewed these shabby conscripts with a distinctly jaundiced eye. All of them were discharged as soon as their services could decently be dispensed with and in the meantime they were allotted all the dirty jobs such as battlefield clearance and burial details, and prisoner handling – with unhappy results.

ORDERS OF BATTLE

THE JACOBITES

The Jacobite Army: Prestonpans, 21 September 1745

HRH Prince Charles Edward Stuart
Adjutant General: Colonel John Sullivan
Lieutenant-General William, Duke of Atholl[1]
Lieutenant-General James, Duke of Perth
Lieutenant-General Lord George Murray

Duke of Perth's Division:
Clanranald's Regiment (Ranald MacDonald of Clanranald) – 200
Glengarry's Regiment (Angus MacDonnell, younger of Glengarry) – 400
Keppoch's Regiment (Alexander MacDonell of Keppoch) – 250

Lord George Murray's Division:
Duke of Perth's Regiment (Major James Drummond) – 200
Appin Regiment (Charles Stewart of Ardsheal) – 200
Locheil's Regiment (Donald Cameron of Locheil) – 500

Reserve (Prince Charles):
Atholl Brigade (Lord Nairne) – 500
Cavalry (Lord Strathallan and Sir John MacDonald) – 36

The Jacobite Army: Falkirk, 17 January 1746

Front Line: Lord George Murray
Keppoch's Regiment (Alexander MacDonell of Keppoch) – 400
1/Glengarry's Regiment (Donald MacDonell of Lochgarry) – 400
2/Glengarry's Regiment (Coll MacDonald of Barisdale) – 400
Clanranald's Regiment (Ranald MacDonald of Clanranald) – 350
Cluny's Regiment (Ewan MacPherson of Cluny) – 300
Cromartie's Regiment (Earl of Cromartie) – 200
Farquharson's Regiment (James Farquharson of Balmoral) – 150
Lovat's Regiment (Simon Fraser, Master of Lovat) – 300
Appin Regiment (Charles Stewart of Ardsheal) – 200
Locheil's Regiment (Donald Cameron of Locheil) – 700

Second Line:
Atholl Brigade (Lord Nairne) – 600 (3 bns.)
Lord Ogilvy's Regiment (David, Lord Ogilvy) – 500 (2 bns.)
1/Lord Lewis Gordon's Regiment (John Gordon of Avochie) - 300
2/Lord Lewis Gordon's Regiment (James Moir of Stonywood) – 200

Reserve: Lord John Drummond
French Picquets[2] (Lieutenant Colonel Walter Stapleton) – 250

Cavalry: Colonel Sir John MacDonald
Lifeguard (Lord Elcho)
Pitsligo's Horse (Lord Pitsligo)
Hussars[3] (Major John Bagot)
Horse Grenadiers (Lord Kilmarnock)
Strathallan's Horse (Lord Strathallan)
Total: 360

The Jacobite Army: Culloden, 16 April 1746
Prince Charles Edward Stuart
Colonel John William Sullivan
Escort Troop (Captain O'Shea) Fitzjames's Horse – 16
Lifeguards – 16

Lord George Murray's Division
Atholl Brigade (Lord Nairne) – 500 (3 bns.)
Cameron of Locheil's Regiment (Donald Cameron of Locheil) – 650
Appin Regiment (Charles Stewart of Ardsheal) – 150

Lord John Drummond's Division
Lovat's Regiment (Charles Fraser of Inverallochie) – 500
Lady Mackintosh's Regiment (Alexander McGillivray of Dunmaglas) – 500
Monaltrie's Battalion (Francis Farquharson of Monaltrie) – 150
Macleans and Maclachlans (Lachlan Maclachlan) – 182
Chisholm's Regiment (Roderick Og Chisholm) – 100

Duke of Perth's Division
Keppoch's Regiment (Alexander MacDonell of Keppoch) – 200
Clanranald's Regiment (Ranald MacDonald of Clanranald) – 200
Glengarry's Regiment (Donald MacDonell of Lochgarry) – 500

John Roy Stuart's Division (reserve)
1/Lord Lewis Gordon's Regiment (John Gordon of Avochie) – 300
2/Lord Lewis Gordon's Regiment (James Moir of Stonywood) – 200
1/Lord Ogilvy's Regiment (Thomas Blair of Glassclune) – 200
2/Lord Ogilvy's Regiment (Sir James Kinloch) – 300
John Roy Stuart's Regiment (Major Patrick Stuart) – 200
Footguards[4] (Lord Kilmarnock) – 200
Glenbuchat's Regiment (John Gordon of Glenbuchat) – 200
Duke of Perth's Regiment (James Drummond, Master of Strathallan) – 300

Irish Brigade
Royal Ecossois (Lieutenant-Colonel Lord Lewis Drummond) – 350
Irish Picquets[5] (Lieutenant-Colonel Walter Stapleton) – 302

Cavalry
Colonel Sir John MacDonald (Fitzjames's Horse)
'Right Squadron'
Fitzjames's Horse (Captain William Bagot) – 70[6]
Lifeguards (Lord Elcho) – 30
'Left Squadron'
Hussars (Major John Bagot) – 36
Strathallan's Horse (Lord Strathallan) – 30

Artillery
11 x 3-pdrs (Captain John Finlayson)
1 x 4-pdr (Captain du Saussay)

Captain Edward Harvey (1718-1778), one of the Duke of Cumberland's ADCs at Culloden. Harvey was first commissioned as a cornet in the 10th Dragoons in 1741. He died in 1778 while simultaneously holding the posts of Adjutant General, Governor of Portsmouth, Colonel of the 6th Inniskilling Dragoons, and MP for Harwich! (NMS)

THE BRITISH/LOYALIST FORCES

British Army: Prestonpans, 21 September 1745

Commander-in-Chief North Britain: Lieutenant-General Sir John Cope
Adjutant General: Colonel Earl of Loudoun (64th Highlanders)

Cavalry: Brigadier Thomas Fowke
13th (Gardiner's) Dragoons (Colonel James Gardiner)
14th (Hamilton's) Dragoons (Lieutenant-Colonel William Wright)
Total: 567 troopers

Infantry: Colonel Francis Lascelles (58th)
55th (Lee's) Foot (Lieutenant-Colonel Peter Halkett) – 5 Coys.
57th (Murray's) Foot (Lieutenant-Colonel Jasper Clayton) – 10 Coys.
58th (Lascelles') Foot (Major John Severn) – 8 Coys
    plus 2 Coys. of Guise's 6th Foot
43rd (Murray's) Highlanders (Sir Peter Murray) – 1 Coy.
Loudoun's 64th Highlanders (Captain Alexander Mackay) –3$\frac{1}{2}$ Coys.
Total: 1,464 rank & file

Artillery: Major Eaglesfield Griffith and Lieutenant-Colonel Charles Whitefoord
6 x 1$\frac{1}{2}$-pdr curricle guns
4 x Coehorn mortars

British Army: Falkirk 17 January 1746

Commander-in-Chief North Britain: Lieutenant-General Henry Hawley
Major-General John Huske

Cavalry: Colonel Francis Ligonier (13th Dragoons)
10th (Cobham's) Dragoons (Lieutenant-Colonel John Jordan)
13th (Ligonier's) Dragoons (Lieutenant-Colonel Shugborough Whitney)
14th (Hamilton's) Dragoons
Total: 800

Front Line:
59th/48th (Ligonier's) Foot (Lieutenant-Colonel George Stanhope)
14th (Price's) Foot (Lieutenant-Colonel Edward Jeffreys)
2/1st (Royal) Regiment (Lieutenant-Colonel John Ramsay)
13th (Pulteney's) Foot (Lieutenant-Colonel Thomas Cockayne)
34th (Cholmondley's) Foot (Lieutenant-Colonel Maurice Powell)
8th (Edward Wolfe's) Foot (Lieutenant-Colonel Edward Martin)

Second line:
62nd (Batereau's) Foot (Colonel John Batereau)
4th (Barrell's) Foot (Lieutenant-Colonel Robert Rich)
36th (Fleming's) (Lieutenant-Colonel George Jackson)
37th (Munro's) Foot (Sir Robert Munro of Foulis)
27th (Blakeney's) Foot (Lieutenant-Colonel Francis Leighton)
3rd Foot (Buffs) (Lieutenant-Colonel George Howard)
Total: 5,488

Highland Battalion[7] (Lieutenant-Colonel John Campbell of Mamore) – 800
Loyalist Brigade[8] (Lord Home, 3rd Footguards) – 700

British Army: Culloden, 16 April 1746

Captain-General: HRH Duke of Cumberland
Commander-in-Chief North Britain: Lieutenant-General Henry Hawley

Escort Troop
Duke of Cumberland's Hussars[9] c.20

Advance Guard: Major-General Humphrey Bland
10th (Cobham's) Dragoons (Major Peter Chaban) – 276 officers & men
11th (Kerr's) Dragoons (LtCol William, Lord Ancrum) – 267 officers & men
Highland Battalion (LtCol John Campbell of Mamore (64th Highlanders) – c.300 rank & file

Front Line (1st Division): Major-General William Anne, Earl of Albemarle
First Brigade
2/1st (Royal) Regiment (Lieutenant-Colonel John Ramsay) – 401 rank & file
34th (Cholmondley's) Foot (Lieutenant-Colonel Charles Jeffreys) – 339
14th (Price's) Foot (Lieutenant-Colonel John Grey) – 304

Third Brigade
21st (North British) Fusiliers (Major *Hon.* Charles Colvill) – 358 rank & file
37th (Dejean's) Foot (Colonel Louis Dejean) – 426
4th (Barrell's) Foot (Lieutenant-Colonel Robert Rich) – 325

Second Line: Major-General John Huske
Second Brigade
3rd Foot (Buffs) (Lieutenant-Colonel George Howard) – 413 rank & file
36th (Fleming's) Foot (Lieutenant-Colonel George Jackson) – 350
20th (Sackville's) Foot (Colonel Lord George Sackville) – 412

Fourth Brigade
25th (Sempill's) Foot (Lieutenant-Colonel David Cunynghame) – 429 rank & file
59th/48th (Conway's) Foot (Colonel Henry Conway) – 325
8th (Edward Wolfe's) Foot (Lieutenant-Colonel Edward Martin) – 324

Reserve
Duke of Kingston's 10th Horse (Lieutenant-Colonel John Mordaunt)[10] – 211 officers & men

Fifth Brigade: Brigadier John Mordaunt
13th (Pulteney's) Foot (Lieutenant-Colonel Thomas Cockayne) – 410 rank & file
62nd (Batereau's) Foot (Colonel John Batereau) – 354
27th (Blakeney's) Foot (LieutenantColonel Francis Leighton) – 300

Artillery:
Commander Royal Artillery (CRA): Major William Belford
Captain-Lieutenant John Godwin
106 NCOs & Gunners
10 x 3-pdr cannon
6 x Coehorn mortars

1   Not to be confused with his younger brother John created Duke of Atholl, after William's attainder in 1715. Rather too old for soldiering he did not play an active part in the campaign.
2   One picquet apiece from the regiments Dillon, Lally, Rooth and *Royal Ecossois* plus the grenadier company of the latter regiment.
3   Originally raised by John Murray of Broughton they were distinguished by wearing fur caps but by very little else until the original aristocratic officers were replaced by hardened professionals from the Irish Brigade, after which they turned into a good reconnaisance unit.
4   New regiment mainly raised in Aberdeenshire after Kilmarnock's cavalry troop had its horses turned over to Fitzjames's Horse.
5   Picquets from Dillon, Rooth, Lally and Berwick and possibly a dismounted element of Fitzjames's Horse, numbers are as reported by the Marquis d'Eguilles, the French 'ambassador' to the rebels.
6   The Marquis d'Eguilles stated that Fitzjames's Regiment was actually 131 strong at Culloden; 16 troopers under Captain O'Shea formed part of the Prince's escort. The remaining 35 probably served dismounted with the Irish Picquets bringing it up close to the same strength as the *Royal Ecossois*
7   One coy. 43rd Highlanders; 3 coys. 64th Highlanders; 12 coys. Argyll Militia.
8   Loyalist volunteer units from Glasgow, Paisley, Stirling and Edinburgh
9   Made up of Austrians and Germans, not to be confused with Kingston's Horse.
10 Not to be confused with Brigadier John Mordaunt.

OPPOSING PLANS

THE JACOBITES

After Prestonpans the Jacobites returned to Edinburgh to savour their triumph and recruit their forces, but eventually they were faced with tough decisions. It is important to appreciate that despite their bombastic claim to be masters of Scotland, their actual position was far from secure. On the credit side they had destroyed the Scottish Command's field army, occupied the capital and set up their own administration in much of eastern Scotland. On the other hand with the exception of the barracks at Inversnaid they had not captured

Officer and serjeant of a regular Highland regiment by Van Gucht. While it is often claimed that the Black Watch played little part in the campaign, two companies fought at Prestonpans and at least one at Culloden in John Campbell of Mamore's Highland Battalion.

A fine study by Mclan of a Highland gentleman armed with one of the Spanish firelocks landed in 1719. Similar weapons were run ashore at Peterhead in 1746 and may have been carried by some of Lord Lewis Gordon's men and the Aberdeenshire regiment commanded by Lord Kilmarnock.

a single garrison or post – a point which was periodically underlined by the guns of Edinburgh Castle. On the contrary the regulars holding those forts not only hindered Jacobite recruiting, especially in the Highlands, but also encouraged and assisted in the raising of what eventually grew into quite substantial Loyalist forces.

Ideally therefore the Jacobites' first priority should have been the consolidation of their embryonic regime in order to establish and afterwards defend an independent Scotland. Unfortunately the external threat was far too urgent. Cope's army had in reality been little more than a reinforced brigade largely made up of raw recruits and a very improvised artillery train. At Newcastle-upon-Tyne however Field Marshal George Wade was overseeing a much larger concentration of veteran troops recalled from Flanders. Therefore notwithstanding the 'nationalist' argument for remaining in Scotland, it was resolved to march south and deal with the British Army before the Loyalists could assume a significant domestic threat.

The celebrated march to Derby, and the successful retreat back to Scotland was undoubtedly a notable undertaking. However, admiration of its technical execution can all-too easily obscure its actual aims and consequences. When the rebel army marched out of Edinburgh on 31 October 1745 it still had no clear objective, but at Dalkeith two options were debated. The Prince favoured the direct approach of marching into Northumberland and bringing Wade to battle as soon as possible, but in the end it was decided to avoid an immediate confrontation and instead by-pass Wade and push south into Lancashire in the twin hopes of triggering an English uprising and winning time for decisive French intervention. This point requires emphasising for although by the time the rebels had reached Derby Prince Charles had convinced himself that London was within his grasp, the other Jacobite

leaders had never contemplated such an ultimate objective. This is starkly clear from Lord Elcho's account of the fateful meeting when the decision was taken to turn back from Derby: *Lord George told him [the Prince] that it was the opinion of Every body present that the Scots had now done all that could be Expected of them. That they had marched into the heart of England ready to join with any party that would declare for him, that none had, and that the Counties through which the Army had pass'd had Seemed much more Enemies than friends to his Cause, that there was no French Landed in England, and that if there was any party in England for him, it was very odd that they had never so much as Either sent him money or intelligence or the least advice what to do… Suppose even the Army march'd on and beat the Duke of Cumberland yett in the Battle they must lose some men, and they had after the King's own army consisting of near 7000 men near London to deal with… that certainly 4500 Scots had never thought of putting a King upon the English Throne by themselves…*

THE FRENCH

French participation in the campaign was governed by two factors. The first, as already mentioned, was that strategic priorities were focused on the campaign in Flanders which obviously limited the resources which

Officer's grenadier cap. This particular example was owned by an officer of the 43rd Highlanders before they adopted a bearskin mounted version. It is however typical of the quality of cap worn by most grenadier officers on formal occasions. Ordinarily it was too expensively decorated to wear in action and instead replaced by a cocked hat.

could be devoted to assisting the rebels and ruled out the large-scale intervention which alone could have been decisive.

Nevertheless the rising clearly had some considerable potential to divert British troops away from Flanders and was therefore worth supporting, but the second and, particularly in the immediate term, more important factor was British naval superiority. The British blockade of French ports was by no means as effective as it would become 50 years later and given the right conditions of wind and tide it was theoretically possible to lift a substantial invasion force across from Dunkirk without being intercepted. Once ashore however it would be impossible to sustain it and effectively it would only be able to fight one battle.

Instead French assistance was, with the exception of one large convoy, limited to whatever could be carried on small fast blockade-runners during the winter when it was difficult for British cruisers to intercept them, and this fact is worth bearing in mind when assessing the defensive capability of a Jacobite Scotland. Ultimately, as the Prince had been warned from the outset, in the long term a rising stood little chance of success unless supported by a French army, but the ability (or the willingness for that matter) of the French to actually deliver and sustain that army was dubious to say the least.

THE BRITISH ARMY

The strategic options facing the British Army were very much simpler and boiled down to seeking out and destroying the rebels wherever they were. It was however severely hampered from doing so by three factors in particular.

In the first place of course, like the French army, it was already fully committed to fighting a major war on the Continent and this imposed its own political and strategic priorities on operations. Cope and his supporters later put it about that he had been pressurised into marching

'Rebellion Rewarded'; a contemporary cartoon depicting the rebels at Carlisle. The men on the right with long coats and cocked hats may be intended to represent the ill-fated Manchester Regiment. (National Galleries of Scotland)

Loyalist volunteers in Edinburgh as depicted by the Penicuik artist. The Cumberland Militia who unsuccessfully defended Carlisle must have looked very similar.

north with inadequate forces by a civil administration which was anxious to see the rebellion crushed before too many of its friends and relations became embroiled in it. In actual fact the real priority was to nip the affair in the bud before it grew to such a scale as to require a substantial redeployment of troops from the critical Flanders front.

Having been defeated at Fontenoy and consequently lost the strategically important fortress of Tournai, the Duke of Cumberland was understandably reluctant to release any of his troops from that theatre and it was not until 23 September that the first of them were landed at Gravesend in response to positive orders from London. On the following day news arrived of Cope's defeat and after some debate it was decided to concentrate the bulk of the available forces (which included the parolled Dutch garrison of Tournai) at Newcastle-upon-Tyne under Field Marshal Wade, while a secondary force under Sir John Ligonier was to assemble in the Lichfield area to guard against the rebels' by-passing Wade, and in time a third army group would also be formed to cover London itself from any French invasion.

These dispositions were essentially defensive, but once active operations recommenced another factor came into play, and this was the British cavalry's chronic inability to undertake proper reconnaissance. Their overwhelming numerical superiority ought to have allowed the British commanders to maintain constant oversight of every move the rebels made, through aggressive patrolling, but in actual fact the reverse turned out to be the case. As a result of lacking proper intelligence of the rebels' dispositions and movements, British strategy throughout most of the campaign was reactive rather than proactive and usually in consequence two or three steps behind.

THE CAMPAIGN

A traditional view of Prince Charles Edward Stewart by Robert Mclan. Although he frequently wore a bonnet and tartan coat during the campaign, there is no evidence that he wore the kilt before going on the run after Culloden.

On 9 November the Jacobite army crossed the border with some 4,000–5,000 men, including around 400 cavalry and rather amateurishly laid siege to Carlisle. Wade by this time had concentrated a considerably larger force at Newcastle-upon-Tyne. The precise numbers available to him are unclear but apart from a provisional battalion of recruits and some militia to garrison the city itself, he had a marching army of no fewer than 22 regular battalions, including 10 Dutch, and three regiments of dragoons, with two other cavalry units on the way. Even after detaching two of his battalions (Price's 14th and Ligonier's 59th) to reoccupy Edinburgh his forces ought to have been more than adequate to deal with the rebels but unfortunately an attempt to cross the northern Pennines foundered in frost and snow at Hexham after four terrible days.

The Dutch

In accordance with a 1713 treaty of mutual assistance the Dutch provided substantial reinforcements in the shape of the former garrison of Tournai – captured and subsequently paroled by the French in May. Commanded by General Schwartzenberg, they served with Wade's army until early December 1745 when the arrival of French troops in Scotland rendered their continued employment incompatible with the terms of their parole.

Regiments
Hirzel (Swiss) – 3 battalions
Villatre – 2 battalions
Holstein Gottorp – 2 battalions
Patot – 2 battalions
La Rocque – 1 battalion[11]
Brackel – 4 Companies

In addition there was a small detachment of artillery that served under Cumberland at Carlisle in December.

In any case Carlisle and its garrison of militia had surrendered to the rebels on 15 November and untroubled by the prospect of running into Wade the Jacobites marched south. Initially they were quite unopposed

---

11   Originally intended to reinforce Cope, but arrived too late and served for a time in the garrison of Berwick.   **33**

THE BRITISH ISLES – MAJOR TROOP MOVEMENTS

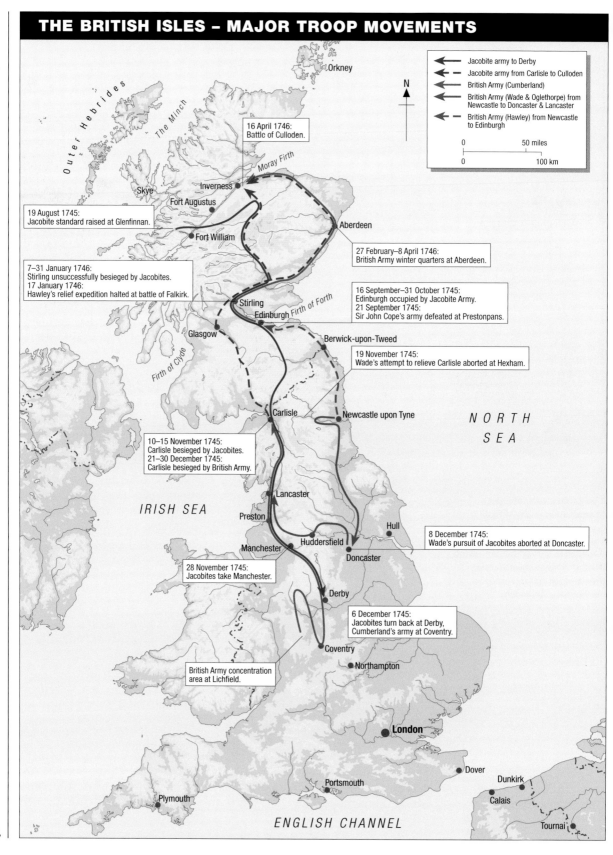

Jacobite army to Derby

Jacobite army from Carlisle to Culloden

British Army (Cumberland)

British Army (Wade & Oglethorpe) from Newcastle to Doncaster & Lancaster

British Army (Hawley) from Newcastle to Edinburgh

0   50 miles

0   100 km

N

Orkney

Outer Hebrides

The Minch

Skye

Inverness

Fort Augustus

Fort William

Moray Firth

16 April 1746:
Battle of Culloden.

19 August 1745:
Jacobite standard raised at Glenfinnan.

Aberdeen

27 February–8 April 1746:
British Army winter quarters at Aberdeen.

7–31 January 1746:
Stirling unsuccessfully besieged by Jacobites.
17 January 1746:
Hawley's relief expedition halted at battle of Falkirk.

Stirling

Glasgow

Edinburgh   Firth of Forth

16 September–31 October 1745:
Edinburgh occupied by Jacobite Army.
21 September 1745:
Sir John Cope's army defeated at Prestonpans.

Firth of Clyde

Berwick-upon-Tweed

19 November 1745:
Wade's attempt to relieve Carlisle aborted at Hexham.

Carlisle

Newcastle upon Tyne

NORTH SEA

10–15 November 1745:
Carlisle besieged by Jacobites.
21–30 December 1745:
Carlisle besieged by British Army.

IRISH SEA

Lancaster

Preston

Manchester

Huddersfield

Hull

8 December 1745:
Wade's pursuit of Jacobites aborted at Doncaster.

Doncaster

28 November 1745:
Jacobites take Manchester.

Derby

6 December 1745:
Jacobites turn back at Derby,
Cumberland's army at Coventry.

Coventry

Northampton

British Army concentration
area at Lichfield.

London

Dover

Dunkirk

Portsmouth

Calais

Plymouth

ENGLISH CHANNEL

Tournai

and Manchester was famously captured by Sergeant John Dickson of the Duke of Perth's Regiment, his girlfriend and a drummer on 29 November. There the few English recruits who had come forward were formed into the Manchester Regiment commanded by Francis Townley, a Lancashire gentleman who had served in the French army. Only ever some 200 strong it barely served to replace those men left behind as a garrison in Carlisle and notwithstanding its propaganda value certainly did not represent the large-scale uprising which had been hoped for. Nor of course had the French landed, but nevertheless the Prince persuaded his officers to push on southwards in search of both and so come into contact once more with the British Army.

In the meantime the Duke of Cumberland himself had superseded Sir John Ligonier in command of the forces concentrating at Lichfield. When he took up his appointment on 28 November (the same day Sergeant Dickson captured Manchester) he found himself at the head of three battalions of Footguards, nine battalions of the line (Howard's 3rd (Buffs), Sowle's 11th, Skelton's 12th, Bligh's 20th, Campbell's 21st, Sempill's 25th, Handasyde's 31st, Douglas's 32nd and Johnson's 33rd) and four newly raised provincial battalions (Bedford's 68th, Montague's 69th, Granby's 71st and Halifax's 74th). In addition he appears to have had four troops of Ligonier's 8th Horse and three regiments of Dragoons (Bland's 3rd, Cobham's 10th and Kerr's 11th) together with two provincial regiments of light horse (Montague's 9th and Kingston's 10th). All in all they probably mustered a total of 8,250 infantry and 2,200 cavalry, and effectively outnumbered the Jacobites by 2:1 in infantry and 4:1 in cavalry. Cumberland could therefore be justifiably confident of victory once he brought the rebels to battle.

William Hogarth's famous (and in part allegorical) print depicting the departure of the Footguards from London is often offered as evidence of their unfitness to face the Pretender's army should it have marched south from Derby, but it would be unwise to underestimate their ability to stand and fight – and win.

LEFT **Jacobite soldier with Lochaber axe as depicted by the Penicuick artist. While the original sketch is a little unclear this soldier does appear to be wearing ragged breeches rather than kilt or trews and he may therefore represent a lowlander rather than a clansman. Axes of this kind were certainly issued to lowland levies in 1715.**

RIGHT **Identified by the Penicuik artist as 'Shittarluck the younger', this is probably McGhie of Sherlock, 'leader of the Rannochs', who died of his wounds after Culloden.**

The trick, however, was pinning them down. On 1 December the Jacobites left Manchester and crossed the Mersey. At this point they still apparently had two options. They could either continue heading south, or they could avoid an immediate confrontation with Cumberland and instead swing westwards into North Wales which was reputedly a hotbed of Jacobitism. Aware that he heavily outnumbered the rebels Cumberland naturally suspected that they would follow the latter course and when the inexperienced 10th Horse came galloping in with the news that they had sighted a mixed body of cavalry and infantry at Congleton on 2 December, he took this as confirmation. In fact had the 10th done their job properly and maintained contact with the rebels they would actually have found the rest of them moving on to Macclesfield, from where they marched south-eastwards to Leek on 3 December and entered Derby on the afternoon of 4 December. Cumberland, meanwhile having vainly waited to intercept them at Stone in Staffordshire now began a forced march in order to head them off. He confidently anticipated bringing them to battle in the Northampton area, well short of London, and by 6 December was approaching Coventry when he received the unexpected news that they had turned back.

The Jacobite leaders' decision to retire from Derby was an entirely rational one which did not proceed from a failure of nerve but rather the all too sensible realisation of the desperate danger in which they stood.

Decision at Derby

At this point in time the Duke of Cumberland had a pretty good idea of the strength and composition of the rebel army, but was having some difficulty in establishing their whereabouts and movements. The Jacobites on the other hand had a pretty good idea of Cumberland's position and knew or correctly anticipated there was probably another

Highland gentleman apparently incongrously but entirely accurately depicted by Mclan riding a Shelty or Highland pony. Ordinarily such ponies were a popular means of transport over boggy ground, but in 1715 one Jacobite cavalry unit was unkindly alleged to have been mounted on ponies.

army covering London. What they did not know was the strength of either force. Now, quite dramatically, they found out.

Before leaving Congleton Lord George Murray had sent a patrol of Lord Kilmarnock's Horse Grenadiers off towards Newcastle-under-Lyme. Just north of the little town they surprised a party of Dragoons at the *Red Lion* in Talke. The troopers promptly mounted and ran and in the confusion managed to leave behind a certain 'Captain' John Vere. Actually a Lieutenant in the 9th Marines, Vere was one of the intelligence officers operating out of Edinburgh Castle and had been shadowing the Jacobites ever since they first raised their standard at Glenfinnan. It did not take the rebels long to realise whom they had caught and disregarding enthusiastic suggestions that he should be strung up on the spot, Murray brought him up to headquarters at Derby for interrogation and thus learned for the first time just how strong Cumberland's army really was.

A council of war was hastily convened at which Murray forcefully declared the expedition had been launched in the hope of triggering an

TOP **Outdated and in poor repair the fortifications of Carlisle Castle were still strong enough to resist all but the heaviest of guns and it was demoralisation of the garrison rather than artillery fire which brought about its surrender in both sieges during the rising.**

ABOVE **Carlisle Cathedral – under the terms of their surrender to Cumberland's forces the Jacobite garrison marched out of the castle and assembled here for processing.**

English uprising or co-operating with a French invasion force. Neither had materialised and instead a confrontation with two numerically superior forces was imminent. Unsurprisingly all the officers present voted for an immediate retreat, to the fury of the Prince who had succeeded in convincing himself that it was only necessary for him to simply set foot in London – now perhaps only three days away – in order to accomplish a second Restoration.

Instead early on the morning of 6 December the rebels began retracing their steps but it was not until late afternoon that Cumberland, then north of Coventry, learned of the fact and set off in pursuit with all his cavalry and just 1,000 hastily mounted infantry. Of itself this force was clearly too small to accomplish much but he hoped to be able to hang on the Jacobites' coattails and slow them down long enough for Wade's army to throw itself across their path. Wade, however, slow and indecisive as ever, was still in Yorkshire. On 8 December when he received Cumberland's orders his cavalry were at Doncaster while his infantry were still trailing far behind at Ferrybridge. Turning west he was in Wakefield two days later, but by then the rebels were in Manchester and there was no prospect at all of his getting ahead of them. Giving up, he turned around and began retracing his steps to Newcastle-upon-Tyne, but not before detaching a cavalry brigade under Brigadier General James Oglethorpe to continue the pursuit.

After a 17-mile march the rebels got to Preston on the night of 11 December, well ahead of Oglethorpe and his men at Huddersfield, but their apparent mobility was illusory. While they were certainly capable of impressive bursts of speed marching, these were invariably followed by a day of rest to recover. Tactically this had enabled them to confuse and evade their opponents during the southwards march, but now that they were committed to the long haul back up the road to Scotland it was a different matter, and the steadier but more relentless pace of the regulars began to tell.

On 13 December Oglethorpe, having added Kingston's 10th Horse to his force, moved into Preston just hours behind the rebel rearguard. Shortly afterwards Cumberland himself turned up and the Georgia Rangers were pushed forward to Garstang. The Rangers were a small mounted infantry unit comprising just two troops of 60 men, specifically recruited for service in the recently established colony. They had actually been embarked for America when they were diverted north to join Wade's army and intriguingly contemporary newspaper reports also mention that they were accompanied by an Indian 'king'. They were ideally suited to scouting and soon one of their patrols, 'cload in green with leather caps', clashed with a Jacobite reconnoitring party led by Sullivan and Murray. In a brief little skirmish two of the Rangers were taken prisoner and revealed the unwelcome news that Cumberland was at hand.

Until that moment the Jacobites had been planning to fight Oglethorpe before any support could reach him, but now they retired at once and for a time contact was broken, since Cumberland, to his dismay, received peremptory orders to fall back on London to deal with a French landing. Next day, to his relief, the orders were counter-manded since the supposed invasion turned out to be a false alarm and on the night of 17 December Oglethorpe again caught up with the rebels at Shap. Apprised of this and correctly deducing that it could only be a rearguard Cumberland sent orders for Oglethorpe to dismount his men and attack the village at once. Unfortunately, in the meantime the Brigadier had already decided against such a desperate undertaking, turned off the road and ensconced his brigade in the village of Orton for the night. Consequently not only did Cumberland's messenger fail to locate him, but next morning he and his men actually rejoined the road behind the Duke. Unsurprisingly Cumberland was furious and expressing himself accordingly, he relieved Oglethorpe of his command on the spot and subsequently had him cashiered.

Clifton

Nevertheless the Jacobite rearguard was still in considerable danger of being cut off. At about midday the Georgia Rangers managed to get between the rearguard and the main body and although they were

Highland piper by Bowles; one of a well-known series depicting the Black Watch mutineers of 1743. The same figure can be seen re-used in *Rebellion Rewarded.*

A useful illustration by McIan of the *philabeg* or little kilt, first introduced in the 1720s and ironically only really popularised by the British Army's Highland regiments in the years after Culloden. The painting may be intended to represent Lord George Murray.

Angus McDonnell, younger of Glengarry. Colonel of Glengarry's Regiment he was accidentally shot dead after the battle of Falkirk and the regiment consequently suffered a disproportionately high desertion rate.

brushed aside Cumberland finally caught up at the little village of Clifton. Initially he drew up both cavalry brigades on the open expanse of Clifton Moor, an area of common grazing, but as the light failed at about four in the afternoon he dismounted his dragoons and ordered them to advance through some hedged enclosures to assault the rebels grouped around the village itself.

Lord George Murray, commanding the rearguard, had sent off for reinforcements but instead received orders to fall back at once on Penrith. Rightly judging it was too late for that, and wrongly concluding there were only some 500 dismounted dragoons approaching the village, he decided to launch a hasty counter-attack.

On the west side of the road (his right) he had Glengarry's Regiment, while John Roy Stuart's Regiment lay astride it in front of the village, and two other battalions led by Cluny Macpherson and Stewart of Ardsheal were drawn up on the eastern side. Murray went in with Cluny's men and succeeded in forcing Bland's 3rd Dragoons to fall back, but the other regiments got into a firefight with Cobham's 10th and Kerr's 11th Dragoons and made no progress at all. After a few minutes therefore the rebels retired under cover of darkness and proclaimed a famous victory with upwards of 100 dragoons down for the loss of just 12 of their own men wounded. In reality only 10 dragoons were killed (and afterwards buried in Clifton churchyard) and a few wounded, and five Jacobites were left behind dead on the field. Rather more ominously from the rebels' point of view, had they considered it, was the fact that the regulars had not obligingly run away when faced by a Highland charge.

Nevertheless the action was successful in that the Jacobites again managed to break contact and, having left a garrison in Carlisle, re-crossed the border into Scotland on 20 December. Ostensibly its purpose was to hold open a gateway for a renewed incursion into England, but this can have been no more than a cynical encouragement to the doomed defenders. Their real task was to delay Cumberland, which they succeeded in doing until 30 December.

Oddly enough when the garrison, largely comprising detachments of the Duke of Perth's, John Roy Stuart's and Lord Ogilvy's regiments, surrendered the ubiquitous Captain Vere turned up and this time would

Unidentified dragoon guidon with a sharply cut swallow tail is typical of the period. This particular example was captured in Flanders but it usefully illustrates the lack of regulation at this time. A 13th Dragoon guidon taken at Falkirk and subsequently carried by Lord Balmerino's troop of Lifeguards bore the motto Britons Strike Home.

ABOVE **Unidentified colour taken at Culloden; the motto is associated with the Kinloch family and the colour may therefore have been carried by Sir David Kinloch's 2nd Battalion of Lord Ogilvy's Regiment. If so it was probably the one thrown away by Ensign James Stormonth as he fled from Falkirk.**

ABOVE, LEFT **Doune Castle, near Dunblane. Notwithstanding its dilapidated condition it was used by the Jacobites to house prisoners of war from Falkirk in 1746.**

have been hung as a deserter by the British Army had he not been able to obtain confirmation from Edinburgh of his true status!

The rebels meanwhile had returned to Scotland to face an interesting strategic situation. They had no sooner abandoned Edinburgh exactly two months before than it was reoccupied by a brigade marched up from Berwick by Brigadier-General Handasyde. Briefly appointed Commander-in-Chief, North Britain, Handasyde was an energetic officer who supplemented his regular battalions with a regularly enlisted provincial battalion raised in Edinburgh, two more Loyalist volunteer battalions raised in Glasgow and Paisley and a fourth from Stirling. Thus reinforced he was able to hold the Forth Crossings and so prevent a second Jacobite army led by Lord John Drummond from marching south to join the Prince's army. Such a junction only became possible once the arrival of the latter at Glasgow rendered the continued defence of the Forth untenable, and at that point the Loyalist brigade, commanded by the Earl of Home, retired with the regulars on Edinburgh.

By now the weather was becoming the dominant factor in determining strategy on both sides. Cumberland was temporarily recalled to London, but Lieutenant-General Henry Hawley superseded Wade at Newcastle and was appointed CinC, North Britain. His first priority was to secure Edinburgh, but hampered by bad weather and a shortage of accommodation on the road he could only feed up two battalions at a time and did not complete his concentration there until 10 January. In the meantime the Jacobites, also recognising the need to establish a proper base of their own for the winter, decided to seize the strategically important town of Stirling.

Embarrassingly, the burgh's loyalist militia initially defied the rebels, but even after they eventually agreed to surrender, the castle above them still held out, forcing the Jacobites to undertake an inept and ultimately futile siege. Within the week Hawley was on the march.

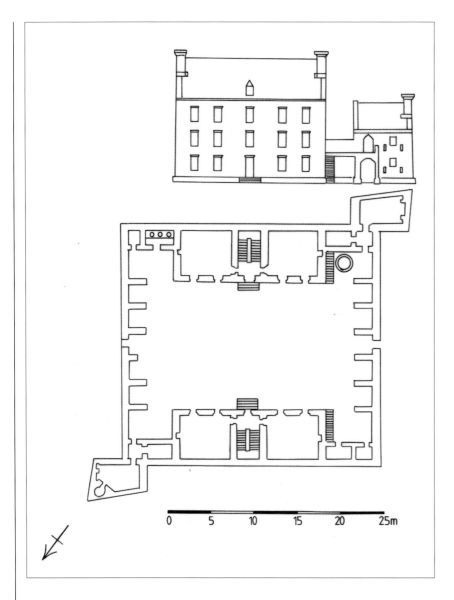

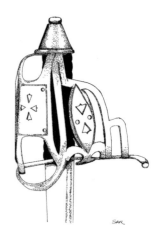

Plan and elevation of Ruthven Barracks, Kingussie. Each of the two barrack blocks was capable of housing an entire company, and there was adjacent stabling for a troop of dragoons, but when the rebels attacked in August 1745 it was defended only by Sergeant Molloy and 12 men. Promoted to a lieutenancy in recognition of his determination, Terry Molloy had to surrender when the Jacobites brought up artillery in February.

Government pattern broadsword hilt. This particular type, which was issued to the rank and file of regular highland units such as the Black Watch, although very much cruder and plainer than the example on page 8 is unmistakeably of the Glasgow style.

FALKIRK

The arrival of Lord John Drummond and his men in Scotland had forced the withdrawal of the Dutch contingent, still prevented by the terms of their parole from fighting against French troops, but notwithstanding Hawley still had three regiments of Dragoons, numbering about 800 troopers, 12 battalions of regular infantry totalling 5,488 officers and men, with another 1,500 loyalists and a rather scratch train of artillery. Hearing that he was on his way, the Jacobites scaled down their siege and prepared to meet him on nearby Plean Moor. Unfortunately, the meeting was delayed, for Hawley, unwilling to patrol aggressively with his cavalry, moved forward very cautiously and encamped at Falkirk where he was joined on 17 January by the Argyll Militia. This slow approach created a very real problem for the rebels. It was after all the middle of January and as they very quickly

OPPOSITE **Dr Archie Cameron; Locheil's younger brother and the lieutenant-colonel of his regiment served right through the Rising from the raising of the standard at Glenfinnan to the final debacle at Muirlaggan. Fleeing to France he returned to Scotland in 1753 in an attempt to recover what remained of the French gold landed at Loch nan Uamh, but was betrayed – probably by those who had it – and executed.**

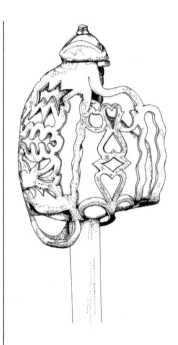

In contrast to the very traditional Glasgow style of hilt, Stirling-made hilts were much freer in design and often cast in brass rather than steel. This particular example, although typical, is relatively restrained.

Unidentified colour included in the list of trophies taken at Culloden; the motto is associated with the Sinclair family, but unfortunately no-one of that name is known to have held a higher rank than captain in the Jacobite army. It may therefore be a relic of the Rising of 1715 pressed into service again, possibly by Cromartie's Regiment, in which case it will have been taken at Embo rather than Culloden.

realised the weather conditions made it quite impossible to keep the army concentrated in the open. In short, faced with the unpalatable prospect of dispersing again and then running the danger of being cut up in detail, they took the soldier-like decision to go on to the offensive themselves.

Three battalions under the Duke of Perth and Gordon of Glenbuchat were left behind to maintain the blockade of Stirling, but the greater part of the army, comprising the Highland Division under Lord George Murray, and a number of Lowland units intended to form a second line were committed to the operation. Lord John Drummond with the cavalry and a composite battalion of French regulars comprising the grenadier company and a picquet drawn from his own *Royal Ecossois* and the three Irish picquets was initially sent off by a different route by way of a diversion, but on his rejoining the total strength of the rebel army came to something in the region of 5,800 infantry and 360 cavalry.

Hawley, for his part, had totally underestimated his opponents and this move took him completely by surprise. Warned just in time by a loyalist scout named Sprewel, he got his army moving and galloped up on to the nearby Hill of Falkirk which overlooked his position. From there it quickly became apparent that the Jacobites were equally aware of its importance and a desperate race began to secure the summit. Hawley's three cavalry regiments, commanded by Colonel Francis Ligonier, reached the top first, but the infantry (formed in two lines each of six battalions) were still lagging behind, so in order to gain time Hawley ordered Ligonier to immediately charge the rebel right wing without waiting for support.

As some of them afterwards admitted the unexpected appearance of the dragoons caused dismay amongst the rebels, and the Jacobite front rank immediately fired a hasty volley at long range, seemingly without doing any damage. However, another volley delivered by the second rank at point-blank range was much more effective and a loyalist volunteer named Corse recalled seeing 'daylight' appear in the Dragoons' ranks. The greater part of Cobham's 10th and Ligonier's 13th Dragoons immediately swerved aside, although a number of the former pressed on and burst straight through one of the MacDonald battalions to rout Lord Ogilvy's men who were standing in the second line. So far so good, but Hamilton's 14th Dragoons had simply turned around and bolted straight back down their side of the hill, and in the process they rode over the loyalist Glasgow Volunteers, who quite understandably responded by shooting them up.

Disregarding Lord George Murray's orders to stand fast, all four MacDonald battalions then scattered in pursuit and at the same time the rest of the rebel front line surged forward. Just as they came flooding over the crest a wild storm broke, blowing hard in the faces of Hawley's infantry still toiling up the hill. In the circumstances it is perhaps hardly surprising that some of them panicked and ran without firing a shot.

To all appearances the Jacobites were on the point of winning a dramatic victory, but tellingly it was only the outflanked regiments of the left wing – Edward Wolfe's 8th, Blakeney's 27th and Monro's 37th – who actually broke and so suffered the heaviest casualties. Some of the regiments in the centre also retired with indecent haste, but they pretty well escaped unscathed and soon recovered their composure at the bottom of the hill.

They were able to do so because, blind to each other's positions as they climbed the hill, the two armies were badly misaligned and while the MacDonalds and Locheil's Camerons outflanked Hawley's left, the British right wing similarly outflanked the Jacobite left. Now, amidst all the confusion Brigadier-General James Cholmondley ordered Barrell's 4th and Ligonier's 59th to swing backwards and pour a succession of volleys into the rebels' exposed flank.

This brought about an immediate and dramatic change of fortunes as the rebels first stumbled to a confused halt and amidst the customary cries of treachery ran away in their turn. As Colonel Sullivan disgustedly recalled, '…the cursed hollow square came up, took our left in flanc & obliged them to retire in disorder. There was no remedy nor succor to be given them. The second ligne, yt HRHs counted upon, went off, past the river & some of them even went to Bannockburn, & Sterling, where they gave out yt we lost the day'.

They very nearly did, for not only had half of the front line and greater part of the second line run away, but Cholmondley was soon joined by some of the dragoons and Major-General Huske also brought up three more battalions. Thus encouraged the brigadier proposed a full-scale counter-attack, but he was overruled by Huske, who wanted to wait for Brigadier Mordaunt to bring up the rest of the army from the bottom of the hill. By contrast in the meantime Lord George Murray was having no success whatever in recalling the MacDonalds, although Colonel Sullivan eventually managed to bring up the French Picquets, who by this time were the only formed body of Jacobites still on the field. With both darkness and heavy rain falling, and no real sign of the opposing army, Huske prudently declined to engage this little battalion and instead retired back to the camp.

For a time Hawley considered holding his position there, for by now he and Mordaunt had rallied most of his runaways. It was in fact an old Roman campsite, still surrounded by the remains of earthworks and should have been defensible, but in the darkness and driving rain no-one had much stomach for it, so he fell back first to Linlithgow and then to Edinburgh. This gave the Jacks sufficient excuse to claim a famous victory, but in reality it had been a rerun of Sherriffmuir in 1715 where it was famously said that 'We ran and they ran, and everybody ran away man.' Neither side had actually suffered many casualties. The Jacobites admitted to some 50 killed and 60–80 wounded, while the British Army apparently lost about 70 killed, although that included 20 officers. This unusually high proportion of officers killed, as they readily admitted, was simply down to their having been deserted by their men and most of the officer casualties belonged to the three regiments; Wolfe's 8th, Blakeney's 27th and Monro's 37th Foot which were outflanked and broken by the Camerons and Stewarts.

Ominously, however, rumours soon began to circulate that many of those officers were killed in cold blood, including Sir Robert Munro of Foulis, the colonel of the 37th Foot. He was initially wounded and was being treated by his brother, a surgeon, when both were murdered. Munro's case aside there may have been some exaggeration in these stories, but they were remembered three months later at Culloden.

Large numbers of officers and men on both sides had in fact simply scattered far and wide across the countryside, and particularly on

Clansman demonstrating the characteristic Highland style of fencing with the targe or shield primarily used to protect the head while making scything downward cuts with the sword.

Once more his breeches or trews identify this swordsman as a gentleman and his stance suggests a classical training – though this may have been provided by an itinerant dancing master rather than a continental master.

Culloden Moor looking from the British front line towards the rebels' front line as marked by the trees on the horizon.

OPPOSITE **A very fine rear view of a highland gentleman by McIan. In this particular case the bull-hide covered targe or circular shield is elaborately decorated, but many of those issued to Jacobite officers during the rising were hastily knocked up in Edinburgh workshops and surviving examples are very crudely decorated.**

the Jacobite side were afterwards slow to return to the colours. Consequently, despite putting it about that they had won the battle, there was no pursuit by the rebels and no real elation at their pretended victory. By contrast, although the British Army was under no illusions that it had won the battle, neither its officers nor its men considered themselves to have been beaten. When dried out and resupplied, they marched westwards again. The rebels declined to fight and instead raised the siege of Stirling Castle and retired northwards.

From this point on the Jacobites' aim was to avoid major operations until the spring brought in fresh recruits, and hope that in the meantime dark nights and dirty weather would help French blockade runners to bring both reinforcements and money. In the short term, however, having been turned out of Stirling it was necessary to secure a suitable base and the obvious choice was Inverness. Accordingly at Perth the army split in two.

While the Lowland Division and the cavalry retired up the east coast, through Aberdeen, and after a nightmare struggle through a blizzard, eventually took up winter cantonments behind the river Spey, the Highland Division marched directly on Inverness.

Throughout the rising, the Highland capital had served as the base for a loyalist army, largely made up of Independent Companies and some less formally organised clan levies, all commanded by John Campbell, Earl of Loudoun. On the positive side this army achieved a considerable amount by its very existence and certainly prevented the

47

Jacobites from taking over the area, but its military operations were far from impressive. Loudoun was a good administrator who had served as Cope's Adjutant General, but quite out of his depth when in independent command. Some 10 years after the rising, when serving as CinC North America he would be unkindly compared to the figure of St. George on tavern signs: always on horseback but going nowhere.

So it was in Scotland. The only serious operation mounted by his army was an attempt to recapture Aberdeen just before Christmas 1745. At the last moment Loudoun took himself off on a punitive expedition to the Frasers' country, thus leaving the expedition to be commanded by the inexperienced Laird of Macleod. Rather predictably Macleod made a complete shambles of it and allowed his men to be surprised and routed in a battle at Inverurie on the night of 23 December.

Notwithstanding this debacle Loudoun, on learning that the Jacobites were approaching Inverness, for once took decisive action and set off under cover of darkness to attack the rebel headquarters at Moy Hall. Once again it ended in a farce afterwards celebrated as the 'Rout of Moy'. The advance guard was ambushed by a Jacobite picquet and although no-one was hurt, five of the Loyalist companies at the end of the column promptly ran away and Loudoun then hung around dithering for the best part of an hour before ordering a retreat. In the meantime the Jacobites had also run off and the only positive result of the affair was that the Young Pretender, having bolted in his nightshirt, came down with something akin to pneumonia.

This can have been scant consolation to Loudoun for with the coming of daylight the rebels got on his track and hustled him straight out of Inverness and across the Beauly Firth to the Black Isle.

Having at last secured the base they so badly needed the rebels then set about consolidating their position with a variety of minor operations aimed at finishing off Loudoun and reducing the Highland forts, while covered by the Lowland Division on the Spey.

Cumberland meanwhile had temporarily gone into winter quarters. Leaving a recently arrived Hessian contingent at Perth to cover the Highland roads, he followed the retreating Lowland Division as far as Aberdeen and then in the face of appalling weather put his army into cantonments there for some four weeks.

TOP **Gunner, Royal Artillery, based on a sketch intended to be included in the 1742** *Cloathing Book.*

ABOVE **Officer, Royal Artillery, again based on a 1742 sketch. The fact that he is armed with a firelock is an interesting acknowledgement of his work-manlike role, in contrast to infantry officers who were expected to merely direct the warlike efforts of their men.**

The Hessians

Infantrie-Regiment Garde – 6 companies
Grenadiere Battaillon – 1 battalion
IR Prince Maximilian – 2 battalions
IR Ansbach – 2 battalions

In addition there was a squadron of Hussars (the only one the Hessian army possessed) and a small detachment of artillery.

Although this put an end to major operations, the campaign was by no means closed down for the winter. As soon as he was able Cumberland established a ring of outposts beyond the cantonments and

Partially reconstructed Culwhiniac enclosure wall at Culloden. The modern house in the distance marks the far corner of the wall on which the Jacobite right wing was anchored at the outset of the battle.

pushed a brigade, commanded by Humphrey Bland, out as far as Huntly, in order to cover Lord John Drummond's nearby base at Fochabers. Inevitably there was a certain amount of skirmishing between the two sides, culminating in a heavy Jacobite raid on a mixed party of Argyll Militia and 10th Horse quartered in the village of Keith, halfway between the two, on the night of 20 March but nothing of any real consequence.

Further west the Highland war had begun promisingly enough for the rebels. Ruthven Barracks surrendered on terms on 11 February after old John Gordon of Glenbuchat brought up some artillery; Inverness Castle surrendered with far less excuse on 20 February and Fort Augustus on 5 March, but after that it all started to turn sour. Fort William determinedly held out against a mixed force of Highlanders and French regulars and elsewhere the various other rebel detachments found themselves bogged down in lengthy operations which ought to have been completed within a few days.

A major priority was to deal with the Earl of Loudoun's forces who had by this time retired to Tain in Ross-shire, but as the Earl had very sensibly taken all the available boats with him, the rebels were obliged to march the long way around the head of the Cromartie Firth. This gave Loudoun ample time to ferry his army across to Dornoch. The Jacobites then had to turn back and march around the head of the Dornoch Firth, whereupon Loudoun frustrated them by shipping his men directly back over the firth to Tain. This dodging about was to continue for some time until in the end the Duke of Perth and Colonel Sullivan gathered enough boats of their own for a surprise amphibious assault on

The turf-walled Leanach enclosure as seen from the north corner of the Culwhiniac enclosure. The rebels charged past the walls from left to right. Ballimore's loyalist highlanders probably posted themselves at about here, and the clump of trees on the right horizon marks the position then occupied by Barrell's 4th Foot.

20 March. Despite the first wave getting lost in thick fog and mounting a very resolute assault on the beach they had just embarked from, the operation turned out to be a complete success. Loudoun's forces were not only caught unawares but the fog prevented their concentrating to mount a counter-attack. Instead they fled without fighting, but although some led by Loudoun himself retreated westwards and took refuge on Skye, others retired northwards with quite unforeseen results.

With their work apparently done Perth's men were recalled to Inverness, but fate then intervened in the shape of a French blockade runner which was forced ashore at Tongue, in the very north of Scotland on 24 March. On board was a picquet of the Regiment *Berwick* and £12,000 in gold. Naturally enough the smell of the gold aroused the interest of everyone for miles around. Some of Loudoun's men got to it first but a Jacobite brigade commanded by the Earl of Cromartie was then sent north in what turned out to be a vain attempt to recover it.

Meanwhile further south Lord George Murray had embarked on a series of minor operations afterwards remembered as the Atholl Raid. The Hessians at Perth were themselves covered by a screen of small outposts, manned for the most part by the Argyll Militia, and in the early hours of the morning of 10 March Murray's men captured all of them except Blair Castle, which was held by a company of the regular 21st (Scots Fuziliers). At this point he should of course have called it a day and quit while he was ahead, but Blair belonged to his brother, the Duke of Atholl, and he himself had been brought up there, so injured pride led him to embark on a full-blown siege. This, and fending off the Hessians, detained him for three fruitless weeks and further dislocated the plan to concentrate on the Spey in good time to meet Cumberland's advance.

ADVANCE TO CONTACT

After the affair at Keith on 20 March Cumberland had reinforced his forward base at Huntly and sent the Earl of Albemarle to take command. Designated the 1st Division, this force eventually comprised Cobham's 10th Dragoons and Kingston's 10th Horse, and the First and Third Infantry Brigades. Their orders were to remain at Huntly until 10 April to cover the movement of the rest of the army into its jumping-off positions.

Meanwhile Brigadier Mordaunt with the three battalions of the Fifth Infantry Brigade, and four cannon (all temporarily designated the 2nd Division) moved up to Old Meldrum on 23 March, but the operation proper did not begin until the morning of 8 April. On that day Mordaunt's 2nd Division marched due north to Turriff, while Cumberland with the 3rd Division (Kerr's 11th Dragoons and the Second Infantry Brigade) took Mordaunt's place at Old Meldrum, and Lord Sempill, commanding the Fourth Infantry Brigade, moved to Inverurie.

Next day both Cumberland and Mordaunt moved on to the coastal town of Banff and then with no sign of movement on the part of the

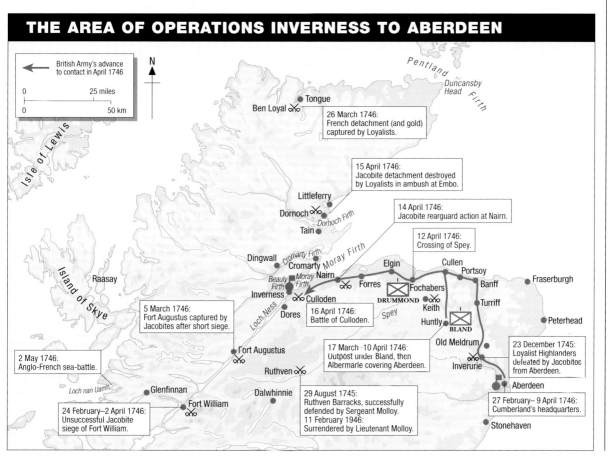

THE AREA OF OPERATIONS INVERNESS TO ABERDEEN

British Army's advance to contact in April 1746

0   25 miles
0   50 km

N

26 March 1746:
French detachment (and gold) captured by Loyalists.

15 April 1746:
Jacobite detachment destroyed by Loyalists in ambush at Embo.

14 April 1746:
Jacobite rearguard action at Nairn.

12 April 1746:
Crossing of Spey.

5 March 1746:
Fort Augustus captured by Jacobites after short siege.

16 April 1746:
Battle of Culloden.

17 March–10 April 1746:
Outpost under Bland, then Albermarle covering Aberdeen.

2 May 1746:
Anglo-French sea-battle.

23 December 1745:
Loyalist Highlanders defeated by Jacobites from Aberdeen.

29 August 1745:
Ruthven Barracks, successfully defended by Sergeant Molloy.
11 February 1946:
Surrendered by Lieutenant Molloy.

24 February–2 April 1746:
Unsuccessful Jacobite siege of Fort William.

27 February– 9 April 1746:
Cumberland's headquarters.

NEMO ME IMPUNE LACESSET

A surviving Jacobite colour, belonging to the 2nd Battalion of Lord Ogilvy's Regiment. (Dundee Museums and Art Galleries)

rebels the whole army concentrated further along the coast at Cullen on 11 April. Fochabers was just a short distance away and not unnaturally Cumberland and his officers anticipated that the crossing of the Spey there would be fiercely contested.

In fact the Jacobites were taken completely by surprise. News that Cumberland had left Aberdeen led to frantic orders for the Highland Division's concentration at Inverness, but the speed of the British Army's advance caught them off-balance. Consequently as Cumberland approached on 12 April, the strong defensive position on the Spey was occupied by only 2,000 men; comprising the cavalry, the Lowland regiments and a little over half the French regulars. They even lacked artillery support but nevertheless might still have been able to contest the river crossing since the ford, as one trooper recalled, was a very bad one, 'having loose Stones at the Bottom, which made it very difficult for Man or Horse to step without falling; the Water Belly-deep, and very rapid; the Ford not lying right across, we were obliged to go Midway into the River, then turn to the Right and go down it for about sixty yards, then turn to the Left, inclining upwards to the Landing Place.'

Instead, covered by a rearguard of Lord Lewis Gordon's men – identified by their white colours – the rebels burned their hutted camp and fell back first towards Elgin and then to Nairn. After weeks of relative inactivity, events were suddenly moving very fast. Hearing that Cumberland was on the move Colonel Sullivan rode out to assess the situation for himself on 14 April and was disagreeably surprised to find Drummond, and his brother the Duke of Perth, actually in the process of evacuating Nairn as well. Uncomfortably aware that the Highland Division had not yet reached its concentration area at Culloden he therefore ordered them to halt and take up a covering position while he himself took the cavalry out on a reconnaissance.

He did not need to go far before he realised the true seriousness of the situation, but in order to give the Drummond brothers time to get across the bridge at the far end of the town he formed up his little force – a troop of Lifeguards under Lord Balmerino, a squadron of Fitzjames's Horse under Captain Robert O'Shea, and the Hussars under Major John Bagot – in a single line in order to make as brave a show as possible. Once across the bridge the infantry formed up and Sullivan, uneasily aware of how badly outnumbered he was, naturally assumed that they in turn would cover his own withdrawal. To his chagrin, however, as soon as he fell back to the bridge they simply turned around and marched off leaving him in the lurch. Fortunately a small picquet from the Regiment Berwick waited for him and 'Sullivan continued his retraite making volte face from time to time alternatively with the small number of horse he had & those five and twenty men of Berwicks.' Repeated calls for more infantry support went unheeded, but after a couple of hours the British cavalry gave over their pursuit and fell back on Nairn, where Cumberland had established his headquarters.

Surviving courses of the south wall of the Culwhiniac enclosure, at about the point where it was broken down.

Knowing that a major battle was imminent Cumberland encamped his infantry on a flat area of ground at Balblair, just to the west of the town, cantoned his cavalry at Auldearn a little to the south-east and decided to give them all a day of rest. On the face of it this decision seems rather extraordinary as Cumberland must have known that the rebel concentration was still incomplete and that a vigorous offensive on 15 April would catch them unprepared, but he may have feared that if he did so they might have dispersed instead of standing and fighting, thus committing him to a long summer campaign.

In actual fact despite still lacking several large contingents, including the Earl of Cromartie's men, the Jacobites had decided to stand and fight come what may. While armchair strategists are fond of advocating that they should instead have retired into the hills and conducted a guerrilla campaign, they themselves were under no illusions about their ability to do so. Lord George Murray afterwards grumbled that they had fought to protect their baggage, but in reality they had little choice. They had no money with which to buy food and therefore had to hang on at all costs to the magazine of oatmeal painstakingly gathered in Inverness. Without it they would starve and indeed the clearest answer to those advocating a partisan war is the fact that when the surviving rebel leaders reassembled their forces for that very purpose after Culloden, they were forced to disperse again almost immediately since it was impossible to feed them.

Accordingly, early on the morning of 15 April the rebels drew up in order of battle on an open stretch of moorland above Culloden House. At the time and ever since there has been some debate as to whether they should have been there at all. Unsurprisingly the earliest critic was Lord George Murray who unequivocally declared that 'there could never be more improper ground for Highlanders' and his trenchant opinion has generally been taken at face value by subsequent historians. On the other hand while there is no doubting Murray's intrepidity and shining qualities of leadership, his actual abilities never matched his own conceit of them and his own choice of battlefield reveals his shortcomings.

On learning that Cumberland had crossed the Spey he pitched upon what he regarded as a suitable position close by Dalcross Castle, but riding out to Nairn on 14 April Colonel Sullivan turned aside to reconnoitre 'this famiouse field of Battle' and his criticism of it is worth quoting at some length; ...*it was the worst that could be chosen for the highlanders & the most advantagiouse for the enemy... There is a Ravin or hollow yt is very deep & large yt goes in zig zag, formed by a stream yt runs there... I ask yu now yt knows the highlanders whither a field of Battle, where there is such an impediment as yt Ravin was, wch is impractical for man or horse, was proper for highlanders whose way of fighting is to go directly sword in hand on the enemy? Any man yt ever served with the highlanders, knows yt they fire but one shot & abandon their firelocks after. If there be any obstruction yt hinders them of going on the enemy all is lost; they don't like to be exposed to the enemy's fire, nor can they resist it, not being trained to charge [load] as fast as regular troops, especially the English wch are the troops in the world yt fires best. If I was to chuse a field of Battle for the English, or if they were to chuse it themselves they could not chuse a better, for there are no troops in the the world but what they overcome in fireing, if yu don't go in sword in hand, or the bayonett among them.*

55

Sullivan's reasons for rejecting Murray's site at Dalcross also go a very long way to answering criticism of the decision to fight on Culloden Moor, on the grounds that it allowed the British Army full use of both its artillery and cavalry. Not only does this ignore the fact that earlier in the campaign the Highland army had freely chosen to fight on a flat stubble-covered field at Prestonpans against a British Army which had proportionately far more cavalry and artillery than the one which they would fight at Culloden, it also ignores Sullivan's unanswerable point that in order for a Highland charge to succeed the clansmen actually needed a clear open field on which to run at the enemy. It might also be worth anticipating events to remark that far from charging the rebels at Culloden, the British cavalry was prevented by the topography from intervening effectively until the battle had already been won – and not by Cumberland's artillery, but by his infantry.

First, however, there was to be one last tragic blunder. By noon on 15 April Jacobite cavalry patrols confirmed that the British Army was still at Nairn and showed no signs of moving that day. The Jacobite concentration was still incomplete at this time and some officers had resurrected the notion of abandoning Inverness and retiring into the hills, but when this was again rejected Lord George Murray advocated mounting a surprise attack on Cumberland's camp that night.

THE NIGHT MARCH

In outline the plan was simple enough, but fatally flawed. Murray's proposal was that; '...they Should march at dusk of ye Evening, So as the Duke should not be aprised of it, that he Should march about the town of Nairn and attack them in their rear, with the right wing of the first line, while the Duke of Perth with ye left Should attack them in front, and the Prince Should support the Duke of Perths attack with the Second line'. Unfortunately the rebel scouts had failed to discover that Cumberland's cavalry was cantoned out at Auldearn and therefore perfectly placed to intercept Murray's division – or worse still come in on his rear after he was committed to the assault.

In the event it never even got that far. Having waited until well after dark the rebel army set off from Culloden at about eight in the evening. Instead of marching straight down the road towards Nairn however Murray set off across country in order to lessen the chance of tripping any outposts or picquets. Unfortunately progress was not only slow, but large gaps soon began to open up between the various divisions and indeed the individual units as a succession of obstacles were crossed. It is sometimes claimed that the delays were caused by the 'heavily laden' French troops, but as Murray's one-time ADC, James Johnstone, recalled: 'This march across country in a dark night which did not allow us to follow any track, had the inevitable fate of all night marches. It was extremely fatiguing and accompanied with confusion and disorder.' By the time Murray reached Culraick, still two miles from the point where he was to cross the Water of Nairn and swing around the town, dawn was little more than an hour away. Murray therefore concluded that there was not going to be enough time to get into position before daylight and after an impromptu and sometimes heated discussion the other officers

present, including Sullivan, agreed that the operation should be aborted.

In the circumstances this decision was undoubtedly the correct one, but it almost resulted in disaster. Sullivan went back to inform the Prince but missed him in the dark. In the meantime Murray, instead of retracing his tracks, simply turned off to his left and took his division home by the upper Inverness road, without first taking the elementary step of leaving a picquet behind to ensure that the other divisions followed. Perhaps all too predictably while at least a third of the army was returning to Culloden, the remainder led by Perth and Drummond blithely carried straight on, successfully reached their designated start-line and had begun deploying before realising Murray had gone off and left them in the lurch. According to at least one account they were already exchanging pleasantries with the British picquet line so that their extrication was a ticklish business and it is little wonder that there should afterwards have been such a strong tradition in the Highlands that Murray was a traitor!

Be that as it may the Highland army trailed back to Culloden and shortly afterwards received confirmation that the Redcoats were coming. Unfortunately although there was upwards of 10 days supply of food at Inverness, little or none of it had actually been brought forward to the troops. Consequently large numbers of men had already

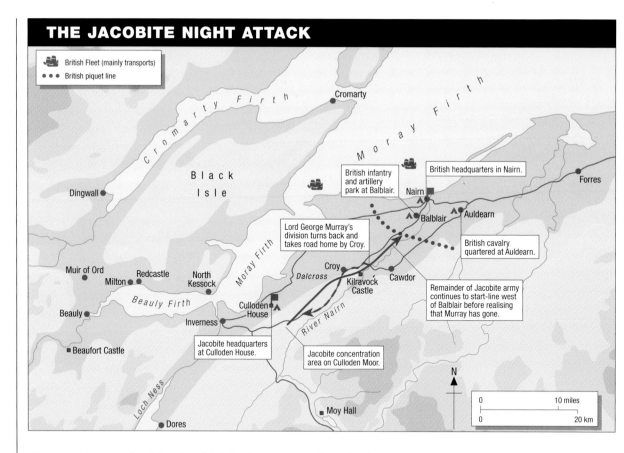

British Fleet (mainly transports)

British piquet line

Cromarty

Moray Firth

Cromarty Firth

Black Isle

Forres

British infantry
and artillery
park at Balblair.

British headquarters in Nairn.

Dingwall

Nairn

Lord George Murray's
division turns back and
takes road home by Croy.

Balblair

Auldearn

British cavalry
quartered at Auldearn.

Moray Firth

Muir of Ord

Redcastle

North
Kessock

Croy

Dalcross

Cawdor

Remainder of Jacobite army
continues to start-line west
of Balblair before realising
that Murray has gone.

Milton

Kilravock
Castle

Beauly Firth

Culloden
House

Beauly

River Nairn

Inverness

Beaufort Castle

Jacobite headquarters
at Culloden House.

Jacobite concentration
area on Culloden Moor.

N

Loch Ness

Dores

Moy Hall

0   10 miles
0   20 km

dispersed in search of food (which had contributed to the late start on the previous night) and now the countryside between Nairn and Inverness was also littered with exhausted stragglers from the night march. It was all too apparent that there were insufficient men actually present with the colours to form a battle-line on their original position and so they had to retire back about a mile to a fall-back position on the plateau immediately above Culloden House.

THE BATTLEFIELD

In 1746 Culloden Moor was a fairly level, if uneven, stretch of common grazing land used by the surrounding tenant farmers. Covered with rough grass rather than heather, it was very wet spewy ground and in some places downright boggy.

The rebel army eventually formed up facing north-east, with its left wing resting on the eastern corner of a series of dry-stone walled enclosures known as the Culloden Parks, being part of the Mains or home farm attaching to Culloden House which lay at the bottom of a long slope stretching down towards the main Inverness road. Forward of this point the moor was wide open, but boggy enough to inhibit movement especially by horsemen – in some places soldiers on both sides would find themselves knee-deep in water.

The moor was rather drier on the other side, where the Jacobite right wing was anchored on a farm called Culchunaig at the extreme western

corner of the stone-walled Culwhiniac Parks. These enclosures stretched down a somewhat steeper slope to the Water of Nairn. Forward of the walls a horseshoe-shaped turf walled enclosure bulged out beside another farm at Leanach. An unmetalled road slanted diagonally across the moor from the corner of the Culloden Parks to this steading at Leanach, seemingly following the limit of the drier ground, for the wettest part of the moor lies to the north of the road.

While superficially the moor appears flat and featureless, losing only 10 metres in height from the Jacobite front line down to the British front line, its variable character still influenced both the dispositions of the two armies and the eventual course of the battle.

Preceded by a Highland battalion – a composite formation made up of elements of both the regular 43rd Highlanders and 64th Highlanders, and the Loyalist Argyll Militia – the British Army advanced from Nairn in four columns: three of them each comprising five infantry battalions ranked one behind the other, and the fourth comprising all three regiments of cavalry. To deploy into order of battle the even-numbered battalions needed only to move out to their left and then forward into the gaps between the odd-numbered battalions in front of them. By this means it was possible to very quickly form two lines each of six battalions, and a reserve of three battalions. This deployment was rehearsed immediately on leaving Nairn and again as soon as they sighted the rebel army. However, when the Jacobites showed no signs of coming forward, the army formed its columns once again and advanced up the moor as far as Leanach, where Cumberland again deployed and this time brought up his guns as well.

Initially his front line, commanded by the Earl of Albemarle, comprised the First and Third Brigades: from right to left; 2/1st (Royal), 34th, 14th, 21st, 37th and 4th Foot, with two 3-pdr cannon placed in the gaps between each. A small battery of light Coehorn mortars was emplaced in front of the second line, commanded by Major-General Huske, which comprised the Second and Fourth Brigades: again from right to left; 3rd (Buffs), 36th, 20th, 25th, 59th and 8th Foot.

Most modern accounts of the battle erroneously depict Edward Wolfe's 8th Foot taking up a rather improbable position forward of and at a right angle to Barrell's 4th Foot on the left of the front line. In reality they remained in the second line until ordered forward during the decisive counter-attack.

Arthur Elphinstone, Lord Balmerino. Commander of one of the troops of the Prince's Lifeguard this veteran Jacobite surrendered after Culloden and was subsequently executed, wearing his regiment's uniform – a blue coat turned up with red. Other descriptions refer to gold-laced hats and red waistcoats.

The third line or reserve comprised Brigadier Mordaunt's Fifth Brigade; 13th, 62nd and 27th Foot and both squadrons of the 10th Horse. The two Dragoon regiments (less one squadron of Cobham's which was off reconnoitring to the north) under Major General Bland were posted on the left of the line, not with anything clever in mind, but simply because it appeared to be the only ground dry enough for them. Once in contact with the enemy the Highland battalion was under orders to rctire to the baggage train, not through any doubts as to their reliability, but rather to avoid any friendly fire incidents. While some of the regulars belonging to the 43rd Highlanders and 64th Highlanders had red jackets, the Argylls had no uniform at all and after Falkirk there even had been a suggestion that they should all be issued with soldiers' hats instead of bonnets in order to readily distinguish them from the rebels. In the event nothing came of it, but while one wing of the battalion, commanded by Lieutenant-Colonel Jack Campbell of Mamore, duly fell back, the other, led by another 64th officer, Captain Colin Campbell of Ballimore, was ordered to remain with the Dragoons.

Ahead of him Bland could see the stone walls of the Culwhiniac Parks and he had a shrewd idea that if he were to get his brigade through them he ought to be able to turn the rebels' flank. In order to do that, however, he needed infantry support. Lieutenant-General Henry Hawley agreed and so the Highlanders were sent forward to tear gaps in the walls.

One of the interesting features of the battle is that in contrast to the rather precipitate way in which both sides set about each other in the two earlier battles, Culloden was characterised by a slow and deliberate build-up and a considerable amount of jockeying for position.

The Jacobite front line originally comprised from right to left: three battalions of the Atholl Brigade (effectively just one large regiment), Locheil's Camerons, Ardsheal's Stewarts of Appin, Inverallochy's Frasers, Lady MacIntosh's and Monaltrie's regiments, a small combined battalion of MacLeans and MacLachlans and another of Chisholms, and three MacDonald battalions commanded by Keppoch, Clanranald and Lochgarry. In total there should have been something like 3,800 men besides officers, but all accounts agree that their ranks were severely depleted by straggling and that there may in fact have been several hundred fewer at the start of the battle.

Initially this line was stretched between the corners of the Culloden and Culwhiniac Parks, but Lord George Murray, who commanded the right wing, became increasingly concerned about the obstacle that the protruding Leanach enclosure would create for any advance. Accordingly he advanced some way down the moor and formed the three battalions of the Atholl Brigade into columns in order to better manoeuvre around it. Although in itself sensible enough, this move was carried out without prior consultation and resulted in some considerable dislocation. It is logical to infer that Murray may have intended thereby to change the axis of the eventual attack in a more northerly direction, since this would carry his men clear of the enclosure when charging straight forward, and as the ground falls away more markedly towards the north he may also have hoped that the downhill run would increase its impetus.

At the other end of the line however the Duke of Perth appears to have misinterpreted his advance as a general forward movement for it must have been at this time that the MacDonalds (who hated Murray) famously refused, despite his urgings, to conform by moving clear of the Culloden Park wall. At any rate with the line now stretched along a rather greater frontage between the corner of the Culloden Parks and a point about halfway down the north-west wall of the Culwhiniac Parks (probably the gate shown on contemporary maps) large gaps now appeared and to his astonishment Colonel Sullivan heard cries of 'Close, close!' and found 'intervals, yt he had not seen before'. In the circumstances there was no alternative but to turn to the second line 'for there was no time to be lost, to fill up the vacansy yt was left (by Ld George's changement)…'

As it happens there was no second line as such. Instead, drawing on the experience of Falkirk, there were simply a number of units scattered along the rear of the first and deployed in column rather than line in order to act as mobile reserves. Again working from right to left there were two battalions of Lord Lewis Gordon's Regiment commanded by John Gordon of Avochie and James Moir of Stonywood respectively, the *Royal Ecossois* commanded by Lord Lewis Drummond, two battalions of Lord Ogilvy's Regiment, John Roy Stuart's Regiment, Lord Kilmarnock's Footguards, John Gordon of Glenbuchat's Regiment, the Duke of Perth's Regiment commanded by the Master of Strathallan, and finally the Irish Picquets commanded by Lieutenant-Colonel Walter Stapleton. Further back still were three bodies of cavalry, a composite squadron

Highlanders (and a lady?) after the Penicuick artist. The story behind this sketch is unknown. It probably records a now forgotten scene observed in Edinburgh during the Jacobite occupation, but it might just possibly represent the Prince, disguised as 'Betty Burke' evading highland militiamen after the rising.

A famous print of the battle of Culloden published by Laurie and Whittle. As is often the case it depicts a number of widely separated incidents and the Duke of Cumberland and his staff are conventionally depicted in centre stage rather than on the right wing as was actually the case.

comprised of Fitzjames's Horse and Lord Elcho's Lifeguards on the right; another formed from Bagot's Hussars, Lord Strathallan's Horse and perhaps some of Balmerino's Lifeguards on the left; and finally a small escort troop of Fitzjames's Horse and Lifeguards with the Prince in the centre.

Sullivan later recalled that he brought forward Perth's and Lord Strathallan's Regiments, but must have been confused by the fact that the first was actually commanded by the Master of Strathallan, for the latter was a cavalry unit, and by the time the redeployment was complete Perth's and Glenbuchat's regiments stood on the extreme left of the front line instead of the MacDonalds, who 'by this had no more the left, they were almost in the Center' and John Roy Stuart's Regiment had also been sent forward to stand beside Ardsheal's men.

These movements did not go unnoticed by the Duke of Cumberland and suspecting, probably correctly, that the axis of the rebel assault was shifting further to his right, he responded by bringing forward two of Mordaunt's battalions, the 13th and 62nd, to extend the right of his first and second lines respectively. At the same time both squadrons of Kingston's 10th Horse were also brought forward from the reserve to cover the right flank and were then joined there by two troops of Cobham's 10th Dragoons who had earlier been sent reconnoitring towards the north.

Meanwhile, Hawley had begun moving through the Culwhiniac Parks in order to try to outflank the rebels. This move had been anticipated by the Jacobites and initially the two battalions of Lord Lewis Gordon's Regiment were set to lining the nearest wall, but as the Dragoons prudently remained outside musket range and may have been

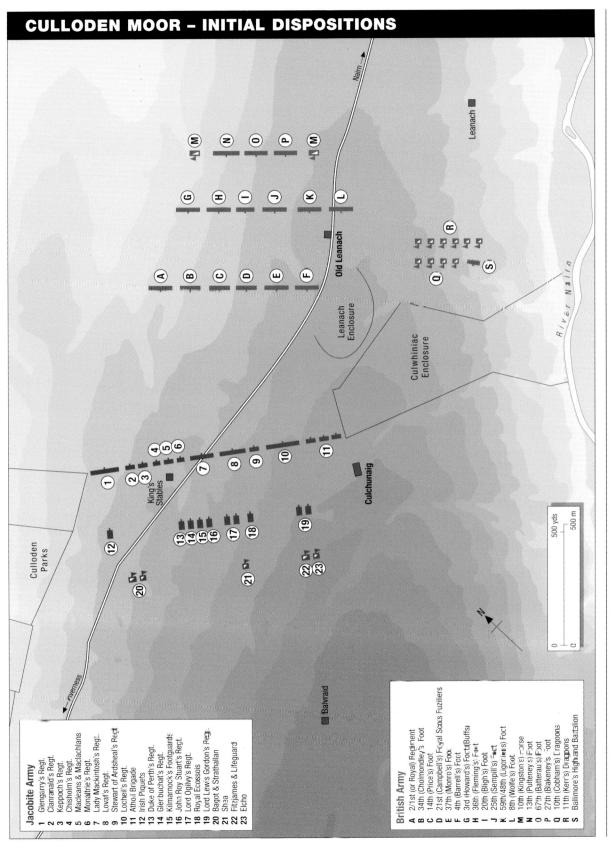

CULLODEN MOOR – INITIAL DISPOSITIONS

Nairn →

Leanach

M   N   O   P   M

G   H   I   J   K   L

Old Leanach

R

A   B   C   D   E   F

Q   S

Leanach
Enclosure

Culwhiniac
Enclosure

River Nairn

Inverness

King's
Stables

4   5   6

1   2   3   7   8   9   10   11

12

13   14   15   16   17   18   19

20   21   22   23

Culchunaig

Culloden
Parks

N

500 yds
500 m
0
0

Balvraid

Jacobite Army

1   Glengarry's Regt.
2   Clanranald's Regt.
3   Keppoch's Regt.
4   Chisholm's Regt.
5   Macleans & Maclachlans
6   Monaltrie's Regt.
7   Lady Mackintosh's Regt.
8   Lovat's Regt.
9   Stewart of Ardsheal's Regt.
10 Lochell's Regt.
11 Athol Brigade
12 Irish Piquets
13 Duke of Perth's Regt.
14 Glenbuchat's Regt.
15 Kilmarnock's Footguards
16 John Roy Stuart's Regt.
17 Lord Ogilvy's Regt.
18 Royal Ecossois
19 Lord Lewis Gordon's Regt.
20 Bagot & Strathallan
21 Sha
22 Fitzjames & Lifeguard
23 Elcho

British Army

A   2/1st (or Royal) Regiment
B   34th (Cholmondley's) Foot
C   14th (Price's) Foot
D   21st (Campbell's) Royal Scots Fuziliers
E   37th (Monro's) Foot
F   4th (Barrell's) Foot
G   3rd (Howard's) Foot (Buffs)
H   36th (Fleming's) Foot
I   20th (Bligh's) Foot
J   25th (Sempill's) Foot
K   59th/48th (Ligonier's) Foot
L   8th (Wolfe's) Foot
M   10th (Kingston's) Horse
N   13th (Pulteney's) Foot
O   67th (Batterau's) Foot
P   27th (Blakeney's) Foot
Q   10th (Cobham's) Dragoons
R   11th (Kerr's) Dragoons
S   Ballimore's Highland Battalion

Highlanders moving into the attack as depicted by the Penicuik artist.

partially in dead ground, they were soon pulled further back and deployed facing due south behind a prominent re-entrant which covered the army's rear near the steading at Culchunaig. As the Dragoons cleared the Parks and swung around to deploy into two lines on the open slope below the re-entrant, further Jacobite reinforcements were hurried up. By the time Hawley closed up to it, the crest above was lined by a total of four battalions from Lord Lewis Gordon's and Lord Ogilvy's Regiments, and the combined squadron of Fitzjames's Horse and Elcho's Lifeguards.

Unsurprisingly, being unable to see what lay behind the crest and perhaps unaware that he had placed himself not on the flank of the rebel army but in its rear, Hawley declined to force a passage across the re-entrant and instead settled down to await events.

As they waited one of Hawley's staff, Major James Wolfe, recorded that the guns began firing on the moor at about one o'clock in the afternoon. Others thought it began earlier, but although there was no real consensus on the hour there was universal agreement that the rebels opened the cannonade. At the outset of the battle they had 11 guns emplaced just forward of their front line. Some sources suggest that they were deployed in three batteries on the flanks and centre, but Paul Sandby, a draughtsman on Cumberland's staff, afterwards depicted a group of four on the right in front of the Atholl Brigade: two in front of John Roy Stuart's Regiment, three in front of Lady Mackintosh's Regiment and the remaining two in front of the Macleans and Maclachlans. It may be of course that they were initially placed neatly

enough but became scattered during Lord George Murray's 'changement'. At any rate all of them were evidently 3-pdrs and there is absolutely no foundation for modern suggestions that their efficiency was impaired by the need to service a multiplicity of calibres.

Nevertheless an analysis of British casualty returns suggests that the Jacobite guns killed or wounded only about 20 officers and men. The Royal Artillery by contrast was rather more efficient although its effectiveness has almost invariably been overstated.

After the Jacobites had fired just twice in a ripple across their front, Captain Godwin's 10 guns (also 3-pdrs) replied. Exaggerated accounts reaching Edinburgh a few days later claimed that the British Army's bombardment went on for over an hour before the clansmen commenced their attack, but this is palpable nonsense. Understandably subjective Jacobite accounts also suggest that they were fired upon for between 20 and 30 minutes, and most historians have accepted this estimate uncritically. In practical terms however an artillery preparation of such a duration would have severely depleted the ammunition actually up with the guns (40 rounds apiece including the reserve in the park) and by contrast British accounts all record a much shorter bombardment. James Wolfe reckoned it lasted 15 minutes, but unable to see what was going on he was relying on sound alone and his estimate must relate to the whole period between the first of the Jacobite guns opening fire and then the British ones ceasing fire because the cavalry were going forward. Similarly, back with the baggage train Campbell of Airds put its total duration at a very precise nine minutes, but those in a position to actually see what was happening told of an even briefer

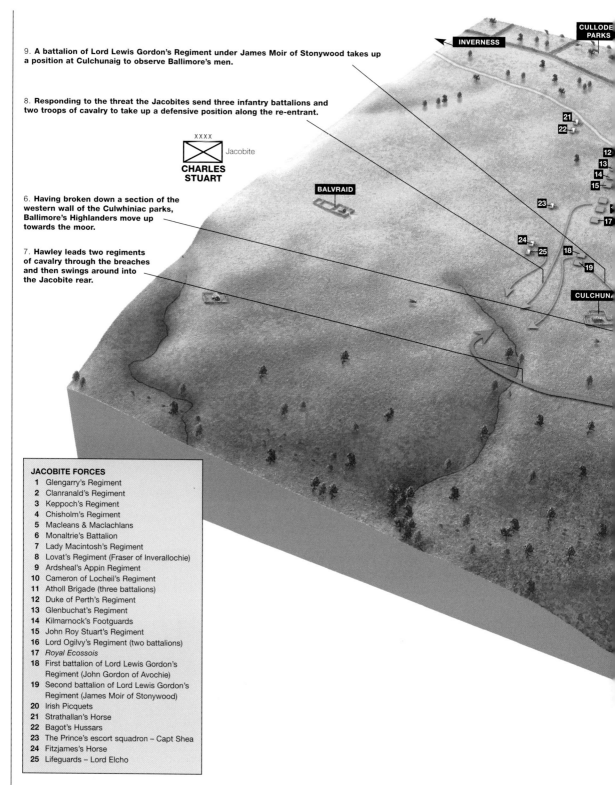

9. **A battalion of Lord Lewis Gordon's Regiment under James Moir of Stonywood takes up a position at Culchunaig to observe Ballimore's men.**

8. **Responding to the threat the Jacobites send three infantry battalions and two troops of cavalry to take up a defensive position along the re-entrant.**

xxxx

Jacobite

CHARLES STUART

6. **Having broken down a section of the western wall of the Culwhiniac parks, Ballimore's Highlanders move up towards the moor.**

7. **Hawley leads two regiments of cavalry through the breaches and then swings around into the Jacobite rear.**

INVERNESS

CULLODE PARKS

BALVRAID

CULCHUN

21
22
12
13
14
15
23
17
24
25
18
19

JACOBITE FORCES
1 Glengarry's Regiment
2 Clanranald's Regiment
3 Keppoch's Regiment
4 Chisholm's Regiment
5 Macleans & Maclachlans
6 Monaltrie's Battalion
7 Lady Macintosh's Regiment
8 Lovat's Regiment (Fraser of Inverallochie)
9 Ardsheal's Appin Regiment
10 Cameron of Locheil's Regiment
11 Atholl Brigade (three battalions)
12 Duke of Perth's Regiment
13 Glenbuchat's Regiment
14 Kilmarnock's Footguards
15 John Roy Stuart's Regiment
16 Lord Ogilvy's Regiment (two battalions)
17 *Royal Ecossois*
18 First battalion of Lord Lewis Gordon's Regiment (John Gordon of Avochie)
19 Second battalion of Lord Lewis Gordon's Regiment (James Moir of Stonywood)
20 Irish Picquets
21 Strathallan's Horse
22 Bagot's Hussars
23 The Prince's escort squadron – Capt Shea
24 Fitzjames's Horse
25 Lifeguards – Lord Elcho

OPENING MOVES

16 April 1746, viewed from the southeast, showing Lord George Murray's 'changement' and LtGen Henry Hawley's move around the Jacobite right flank.

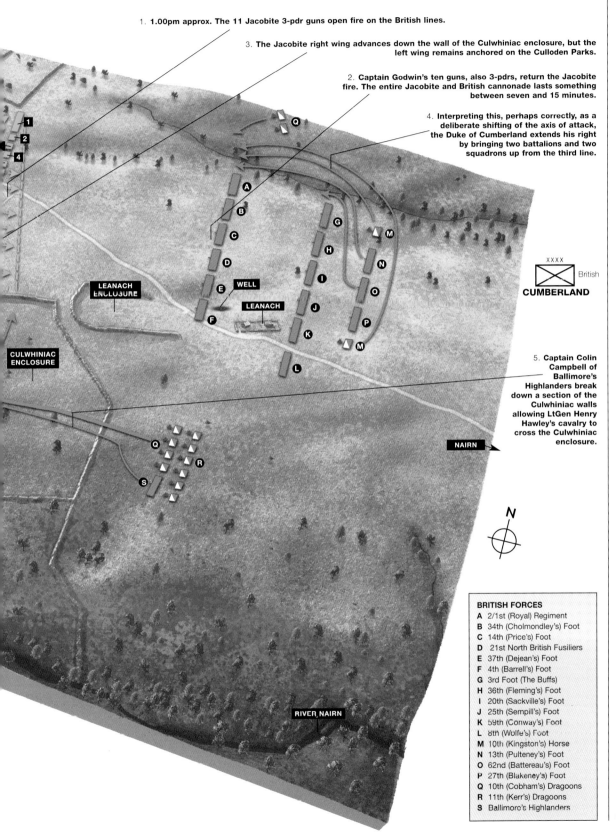

1. **1.00pm approx. The 11 Jacobite 3-pdr guns open fire on the British lines.**

3. **The Jacobite right wing advances down the wall of the Culwhiniac enclosure, but the left wing remains anchored on the Culloden Parks.**

2. **Captain Godwin's ten guns, also 3-pdrs, return the Jacobite fire. The entire Jacobite and British cannonade lasts something between seven and 15 minutes.**

4. **Interpreting this, perhaps correctly, as a deliberate shifting of the axis of attack, the Duke of Cumberland extends his right by bringing two battalions and two squadrons up from the third line.**

LEANACH
ENCLOSURE

WELL

LEANACH

CULWHINIAC
ENCLOSURE

xxxx

British

CUMBERLAND

5. **Captain Colin Campbell of Ballimore's Highlanders break down a section of the Culwhiniac walls allowing LtGen Henry Hawley's cavalry to cross the Culwhiniac enclosure.**

NAIRN

N

RIVER NAIRN

BRITISH FORCES
A 2/1st (Royal) Regiment
B 34th (Cholmondley's) Foot
C 14th (Price's) Foot
D 21st North British Fusiliers
E 37th (Dejean's) Foot
F 4th (Barrell's) Foot
G 3rd Foot (The Buffs)
H 36th (Fleming's) Foot
I 20th (Sackville's) Foot
J 25th (Sempill's) Foot
K 59th (Conway's) Foot
L 8th (Wolfe's) Foot
M 10th (Kingston's) Horse
N 13th (Pulteney's) Foot
O 62nd (Battereau's) Foot
P 27th (Blakeney's) Foot
Q 10th (Cobham's) Dragoons
R 11th (Kerr's) Dragoons
S Ballimore's Highlanders

exchange of fire. Indeed one of Cumberland's ADCs, Joseph Yorke wrote to his father that: 'When our cannon had fired about two rounds, I could plainly perceive that the rebels fluctuated extremely, and could not remain long in the position they were then in without running away or coming down upon us; and according as I thought, in two or three minutes they broke from the centre in three large bodies…'

THE JACOBITE CHARGE

It is in fact relatively easy to estimate the effectiveness of the British artillery preparation. In the first place with the rebel front line between 500 and 700 metres away the little 3-pdrs were operating at the limit of their effective range and with questionable accuracy. The soft ground will have severely limited the 'grazing' effect of roundshot and forced the British gunners to pitch them high in order to reach their target. Naturally enough this resulted in a high proportion of 'overs' and there is ample Jacobite testimony to that effect. It is reasonable therefore to expect that at best they were achieving an average of just one casualty per round fired – and even this may be too high – so with ten guns each firing just one round per minute, a five-minute cannonade is unlikely to have resulted in much more than 50 casualties rather than the hundreds claimed by modern accounts. It was nevertheless the first time the Jacobites had come under proper artillery fire and there is no denying its effect on morale, or perhaps its influence on what happened next.

As a result of Lord George Murray's 'changement' the Jacobite front line was now skewed in such a way that although the right wing was some 500 metres from Cumberland's men, the Duke of Perth's Regiment on the extreme left was more like 700 metres away. Had the Highlanders charged to their left as Murray seems to have intended, they would have by-passed both the Leanach enclosure and Barrell's 4th Foot to strike the British line obliquely.

Unfortunately the required tactical co-ordination was so poor that when Lady Mackintosh's Regiment began the attack by surging forward without waiting for formal instructions, they simply charged straight towards the nearest British unit. Instead of directing their attack obliquely on Cholmondley's 34th, they initially seem to have been making for Price's 14th, and the other rebel regiments on either side also conformed to their direction of attack.

On the other hand, with the Leanach enclosure still bulging out to their immediate front, the three regiments of the Atholl Brigade still found it necessary to move out to their left in order to clear it. Of itself this was going to mean that all the right-wing regiments would become dangerously crowded together, although Murray never seems to have considered holding the Athollmen back from the bottleneck and employing them as a tactical reserve. Perhaps he was unaware of what was going wrong until it was too late, and by then it had gone very wrong indeed.

The decision by Lady Mackintosh's Regiment to charge straight forward was always going to cause problems, but these were suddenly compounded by an involuntary swing much further to the right. As this appears to have coincided with their coming within canister range of the British guns they may simply have been shying away from the fire, but by

now they were also across the road and probably trying to avoid what was obviously very boggy ground.

Whatever the true cause the result of this swerve was that most of the Jacobite regiments in the centre and right wing became entangled together in a huge mob which, despite receiving 5 or 6 discharges of canister and two full battalion volleys apiece from the front line regiments, rolled right down the road and impacted on Barrell's 4th Foot.

Defying precedent neither Barrell's, nor Dejean's 37th Foot standing next to them, ran away. Instead they stood fast, but paid a heavy price. In just a few minutes Barrell's lost 17 killed and 108 wounded out of a total of 373 officers and men, including their commanding officer, Lieutenant-Colonel Robert Rich. Similarly, Dejean's had 14 killed and 68 wounded, although these were disproportionately concentrated in its beleaguered left wing – in fact one of the 37th's grenadier officers related that he had no fewer than 18 killed or wounded in his platoon alone.

Unsurprisingly, Barrell's Regiment was burst apart and effectively overrun, temporarily losing one of its colours in the process, while Dejean's was forced aside and Sergeant Edward Bristoe's gun detachment posted between the two regiments struck was also overrun. This was the critical point in the battle, but by this time the rebel command structure had broken down completely. Had Lord George Murray kept the Athollmen back as a tactical reserve, or the other regimental commanders retained some control over their men, it might have been possible to widen the gap and exploit the breakthrough. Instead more and more Highlanders simply pushed up into the penetration instead of attacking the British units immediately to their front. Given just a little more time they might have been able to work

Culloden Moor as viewed from behind Barrell's 4th Foot – the regiment was deployed just forward of the pond. The trees aside this provides a good impression of the terrain across which the Jacobites charged; relatively flat but far from even grazing land which was (and still is) very boggy in the aftermath of heavy rain.

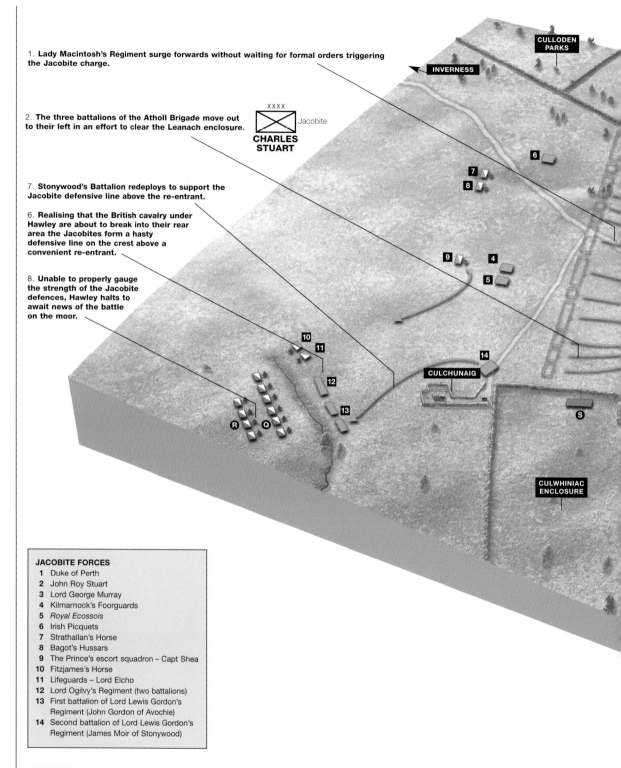

1. **Lady Macintosh's Regiment surge forwards without waiting for formal orders triggering the Jacobite charge.**

2. **The three battalions of the Atholl Brigade move out to their left in an effort to clear the Leanach enclosure.**

7. **Stonywood's Battalion redeploys to support the Jacobite defensive line above the re-entrant.**

6. **Realising that the British cavalry under Hawley are about to break into their rear area the Jacobites form a hasty defensive line on the crest above a convenient re-entrant.**

8. **Unable to properly gauge the strength of the Jacobite defences, Hawley halts to await news of the battle on the moor.**

XXXX
Jacobite
CHARLES STUART

CULLODEN PARKS

INVERNESS

CULCHUNAIG

CULWHINIAC ENCLOSURE

JACOBITE FORCES
1 Duke of Perth
2 John Roy Stuart
3 Lord George Murray
4 Kilmarnock's Foorguards
5 *Royal Ecossois*
6 Irish Picquets
7 Strathallan's Horse
8 Bagot's Hussars
9 The Prince's escort squadron – Capt Shea
10 Fitzjames's Horse
11 Lifeguards – Lord Elcho
12 Lord Ogilvy's Regiment (two battalions)
13 First battalion of Lord Lewis Gordon's Regiment (John Gordon of Avochie)
14 Second battalion of Lord Lewis Gordon's Regiment (James Moir of Stonywood)

THE HIGHLAND CHARGE

16 April 1746, viewed from the southeast, showing the charge of the clans, which slams into the British left flank, smashing Barrell's 4th Foot and Dejean's 37th. MajGen Huske orders Semphill's Brigade from the second line to counter-attack.

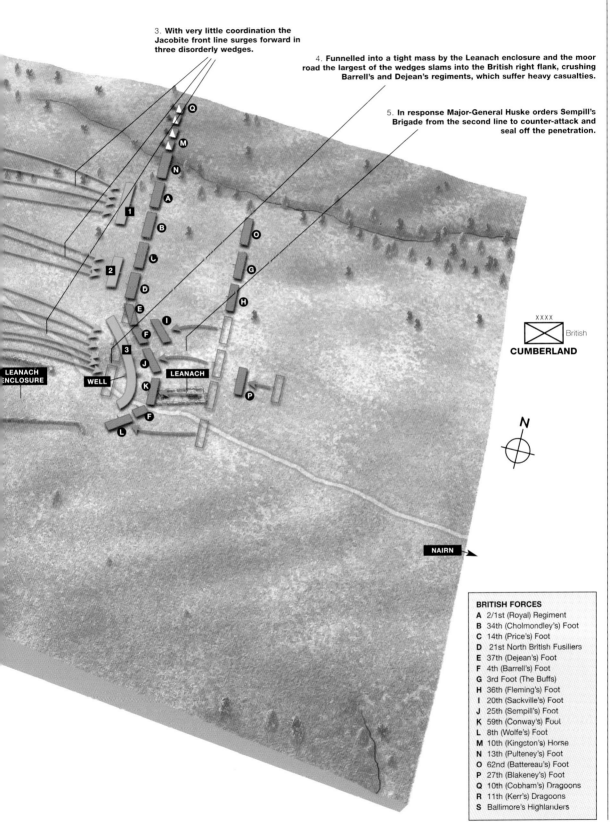

3. **With very little coordination the Jacobite front line surges forward in three disorderly wedges.**

4. **Funnelled into a tight mass by the Leanach enclosure and the moor road the largest of the wedges slams into the British right flank, crushing Barrell's and Dejean's regiments, which suffer heavy casualties.**

5. **In response Major-General Huske orders Sempill's Brigade from the second line to counter-attack and seal off the penetration.**

Q

M

N

A

1

B

C

O

2

D

G

E

H

I

F

3

J

K

P

LEANACH ENCLOSURE

WELL

LEANACH

F

L

N

xxxx
British

CUMBERLAND

NAIRN ➤

BRITISH FORCES
A 2/1st (Royal) Regiment
B 34th (Cholmondley's) Foot
C 14th (Price's) Foot
D 21st North British Fusiliers
E 37th (Dejean's) Foot
F 4th (Barrell's) Foot
G 3rd Foot (The Buffs)
H 36th (Fleming's) Foot
I 20th (Sackville's) Foot
J 25th (Sempill's) Foot
K 59th (Conway's) Foot
L 8th (Wolfe's) Foot
M 10th (Kingston's) Horse
N 13th (Pulteney's) Foot
O 62nd (Battereau's) Foot
P 27th (Blakeney's) Foot
Q 10th (Cobham's) Dragoons
R 11th (Kerr's) Dragoons
S Ballimore's Highlanders

their way around the crumbling flank of the 37th, but the doomed stand by the 4th Foot had already won precious moments for Major-General Huske, commanding the second line, to organise a counter-attack.

Recognising the desperate urgency of the situation he first ordered forward the whole of Lord Sempill's Fourth Brigade, comprising Sempill's own 25th Foot, Conway's 59th and Edward Wolfe's 8th Foot, mustering a total of 1,078 bayonets, besides officers and NCOs.

In order to get into action Sempill's Brigade first had to clear the Leanach steading and what appears to be a preliminary sketch map by Paul Sandby shows Conway's 59th Foot temporarily dividing into two wings in order to do so. Once past the buildings, however, Captain-Lieutenant James Ashe Lee of the 8th Foot wrote in a letter home that, 'Poor Barrell's regiment were sorely pressed by those desperadoes and outflanked. One stand of their colours was taken; Collonel Riches hand cutt off in their defence... We marched up to the enemy, and our left, outflanking them, wheeled in upon them; the whole then gave them 5 or 6 fires with vast execution, while their front had nothing left to oppose us, but their pistolls and broadswords; and fire from their center and rear, (as, by this time, they were 20 or 30 deep) was vastly more fatal to themselves, than us.'

Huske had also sent forward Bligh's 20th Foot from the Second Brigade to plug the gap between Sempill's 25th (Edinburgh) Regiment and the hard-pressed 37th. The result was that all five battalions (and perhaps some remnants of Barrell's 4th Foot as well) were soon formed into a large horseshoe-like arc, hemming in the rebels on three sides.

Culloden Moor; the reverse view looking towards the British lines, represented by the scattered trees in middle distance, once again emphasises that the slight fall in the ground was not militarily significant.

The impetus of their assault having been slowed by the 4th and 37th, the rebel front rank was now brought to a complete halt by Huske's counter-attack, but more and more men came pushing up from the rear until they were all jammed together in one huge immobile column, flayed by a terrible crossfire at point-blank range. British accounts all relate how after their initial battalion volleys had been fired their front-rank men stood fast, or knelt, with charged bayonets, to protect the second and third ranks as they reloaded and fired time and again. If we assume that as little as one round in ten took effect, at this distance a simple calculation suggests that, even allowing for only two ranks firing, around 700 rebels were killed or wounded in the space of just two or three terrible minutes. Chillingly, the macabre outline of their position can still be traced to this day in the great slew of mass graves stretching westward from the aptly named Well of the Dead.

Lord George Murray had lost his horse during the initial assault, but realising that his men would not be able to stand much longer he ran back to hurry forward his own supports. To his dismay there was virtually nothing left.

Popular legend notwithstanding, the MacDonald regiments, far from refusing to charge, had gone forward at pretty much the same time as the others. However, owing to the way in which the Jacobite front line was skewed in relation to the British, they had something like 200 metres further to go and moreover they also had to cross much boggier ground from the outset. In fact James Johnstone, who fought at Culloden as a volunteer in Glengarry's Regiment, afterwards complained that it was not merely boggy but 'covered with water which reached halfway up the leg'.

In the circumstances it is hardly surprising that their advance was so very much slower, or that finding the regulars were not intimidated by

LEFT **Reconstructed 13th Foot: 'Level your bayonets' – the similarity to 17th-century pike drill is immediately obvious.**

RIGHT **Reconstructed 13th Foot: 'Charge your bayonets'. Although this style of bayonet fighting was awkward (and highly impractical) for individuals in a melee, when practised en masse by a formed line it could be surprisingly effective.**

ROYAL SCOTS AT CULLODEN (pages 74–75)
In contrast to the vicious hand to hand fighting and murderous point-blank volley fire on the left wing, the British Army's right wing experienced a much more familiar style of fighting. Far from hanging back, the three MacDonald regiments (1) according to an Ayrshire man named Alexander Taylor standing in the ranks of 2/1st (Royal) Regiment 'came running upon our front line like troops of hungry wolves, and fought with intrepidity. But the thunder of our fire, and the continuation of it, began to slacken their fury...' It was the wet ground that fatally slowed the Highland charge. As is often the case with Scottish hills, the soil on the moor was too thin to absorb the rain and too flat for it to run off. Consequently on the lower slope where the Royals stood, the ground was saturated and covered in pools of standing water. It was impossible for the Jacobites to run and instead as they struggled forward it is likely that the Royals were able to deliver a steady rolling fire by platoons instead of resorting to battalion volleys. As each fired (2) and reloaded (3) in sequence they took a terrible toll of the Jacobite officers in particular. In return they had very few casualties of their own. The Royals had none killed and just four men

wounded. How John Ross came to be disabled by a rupture at Culloden must remain a mystery, unless he did it while hauling one of the cannon out of a bog-hole, but both John Reynolds and Alexander Buchannan (4) were wounded in the left leg – probably by pistol balls.

There were no dedicated medical services and casualty evacuation was almost certainly carried out, as on other battle-fields by the ever-forgotten women who followed the army (5), as one anonymous officer recalled in Flanders 50 years later; 'It would be doing great injustice to the women of the army not to mention with what alacrity they contributed all the assistance in their power to the soldiers while engaged, some fetching their aprons full of cartridges from the ammunition waggons, and filling the pouches of the soldiers, at the hazard of their own lives, while others with a canteen filled with spirit and water, would hold it up to the mouths of the soldiers, half-choked with gunpowder and thirst, and when a man was wounded they would afford him all the assistance in their power to help him to the nearest house or waggon, in which friendly offices it was, as may be supposed, no uncommon thing for the females to get wounded as well as the men, many instances of this kind happening in the course of the campaign.'
(Gerry Embleton)

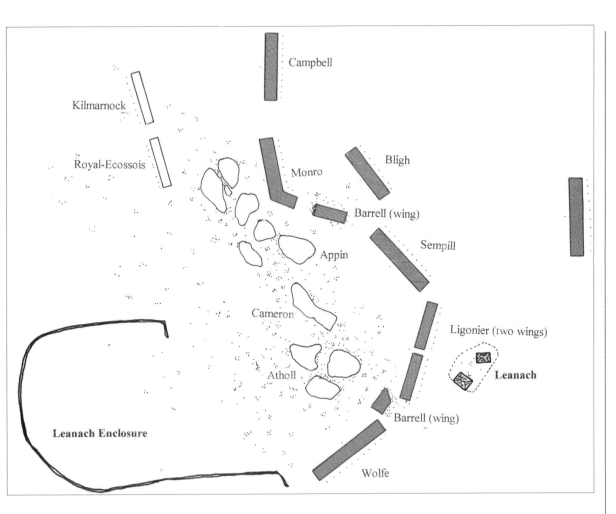

Campbell

Kilmarnock

Royal-Ecossois

Monro

Bligh

Barrell (wing)

Sempill

Appin

Cameron

Ligonier (two wings)

Leanach

Atholl

Leanach Enclosure

Barrell (wing)

Wolfe

General Huske's counter-attack. Initially Huske countered the Jacobite breakthrough on the left by ordering forward Sempill's Brigade (Wolfe's 8th, Ligonier's 59th and Sempill's own 25th) from the second line, but at least one eyewitness account recalled that Bligh's 20th Foot also came up and got into the fight.

their laborious progress, they should have aborted the assault without making contact. Instead they began to fall back. 'Our left flinches,' wrote Sullivan. 'The Duke of Perth runs to Clanronald's Regiment takes their Collors & tells them from that day forth he'l call himself MacDonel if they gain the day. Lord John (Drummond) & Sullivan brings up the left again.' In fact Cumberland himself, having posted himself opposite the MacDonalds, reported that 'They came running on in their wild manner & upon the Right where I had placed Myself, imagining the greatest Push would be there, they came down three several times within a Hundred Yards of our Men, firing their pistols and brandishing their Swords, but the Royals (1st) and Pulteneys (13th) hardly took their firelocks from their shoulders…'

The two small units on the MacDonalds' right – the Chisholms and the combined battalion of Macleans and Maclachlans – pretty well disintegrated. All the officers in the little independent company formed by the Chisholms of Strathglas were killed or wounded, and Colonel Lachlan Maclachlan was fatally wounded by a cannon-shot; an eyewitness gruesomely describing how his 'guts were laid over his horse's neck'. On the other flank Perth's and Glenbuchat's regiments seem to have advanced reluctantly and soon retired, leaving Major Robert Stewart pinned beneath his dead horse. As their leaders were shot down one after the other the MacDonalds too began to give way. Sensing his

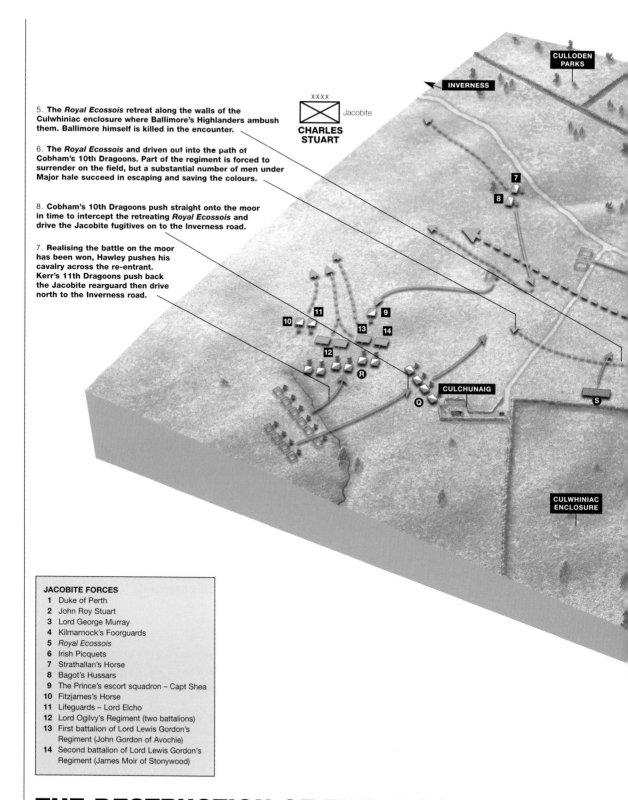

5. The *Royal Ecossois* retreat along the walls of the Culwhiniac enclosure where Ballimore's Highlanders ambush them. Ballimore himself is killed in the encounter.

6. The *Royal Ecossois* and driven out into the path of Cobham's 10th Dragoons. Part of the regiment is forced to surrender on the field, but a substantial number of men under Major hale succeed in escaping and saving the colours.

8. Cobham's 10th Dragoons push straight onto the moor in time to intercept the retreating *Royal Ecossois* and drive the Jacobite fugitives on to the Inverness road.

7. Realising the battle on the moor has been won, Hawley pushes his cavalry across the re-entrant. Kerr's 11th Dragoons push back the Jacobite rearguard then drive north to the Inverness road.

XXXX

Jacobite

CHARLES STUART

CULLODEN PARKS

INVERNESS

CULCHUNAIG

CULWHINIAC ENCLOSURE

JACOBITE FORCES
1 Duke of Perth
2 John Roy Stuart
3 Lord George Murray
4 Kilmarnock's Foorguards
5 *Royal Ecossois*
6 Irish Picquets
7 Strathallan's Horse
8 Bagot's Hussars
9 The Prince's escort squadron – Capt Shea
10 Fitzjames's Horse
11 Lifeguards – Lord Elcho
12 Lord Ogilvy's Regiment (two battalions)
13 First battalion of Lord Lewis Gordon's Regiment (John Gordon of Avochie)
14 Second battalion of Lord Lewis Gordon's Regiment (James Moir of Stonywood)

THE DESTRUCTION OF THE JACOBITE ARMY

16 April 1746, viewed from the southeast, showing the collapse and rout of the Jacobite army and the attempts by some units, including the Irish Piquets and the *Royal Ecossios*, to cover the retreat.

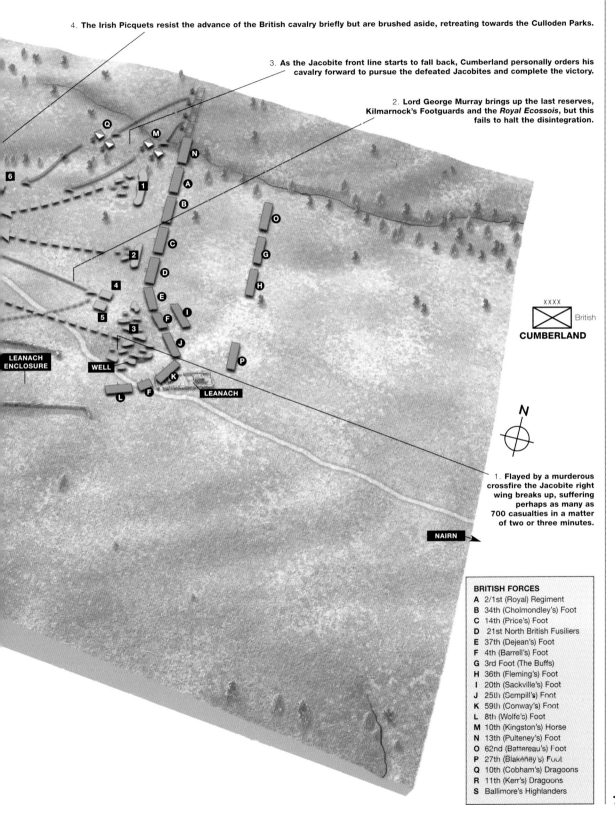

4. **The Irish Picquets resist the advance of the British cavalry briefly but are brushed aside, retreating towards the Culloden Parks.**

3. **As the Jacobite front line starts to fall back, Cumberland personally orders his cavalry forward to pursue the defeated Jacobites and complete the victory.**

2. **Lord George Murray brings up the last reserves, Kilmarnock's Footguards and the *Royal Ecossois*, but this fails to halt the disintegration.**

Q M N A B O C G D H E I F J P K L F

6 1 2 4 5 3

LEANACH ENCLOSURE

WELL

LEANACH

xxxx
British
CUMBERLAND

N

1. **Flayed by a murderous crossfire the Jacobite right wing breaks up, suffering perhaps as many as 700 casualties in a matter of two or three minutes.**

NAIRN

BRITISH FORCES
A 2/1st (Royal) Regiment
B 34th (Cholmondley's) Foot
C 14th (Price's) Foot
D 21st North British Fusiliers
E 37th (Dejean's) Foot
F 4th (Barrell's) Foot
G 3rd Foot (The Buffs)
H 36th (Fleming's) Foot
I 20th (Sackville's) Foot
J 25th (Sempill's) Foot
K 59th (Conway's) Foot
L 8th (Wolfe's) Foot
M 10th (Kingston's) Horse
N 13th (Pulteney's) Foot
O 62nd (Battereau's) Foot
P 27th (Blakeney's) Foot
Q 10th (Cobham's) Dragoons
R 11th (Kerr's) Dragoons
S Ballimore's Highlanders

The victors of Culloden: British regulars as depicted by the Penicuik artist in 1746, presenting a rather different appearance from the elaborately dressed mannequins of the 1742 *Cloathing Book* and David Morier's paintings.

advantage Cumberland himself galloped across to the two troops of Cobham's 10th Dragoons on that flank and according to one of them: 'clapping some of them on the shoulders, call'd out "One Brush, my Lads, for the Honour of old Cobham"; upon which, rather like Devils than Men they broke through the Enemy's Flank and a total Rout followed.'

It wasn't quite as dramatic as that of course, for the dragoons had to carefully splash their way across some very boggy ground indeed so that the MacDonalds may already have begun withdrawing down the Inverness road before they cleared it. Instead they attacked the Irish Picquets, whom Sullivan appears to have brought up in an attempt to stabilise the deteriorating situation on that flank. Exactly what happened next is a touch obscure. A French engineer officer named Du Saussey turned up at about the same time with a field gun – probably a light 'Swedish' 4-pdr – to support them, but Sullivan simply says that 'Stapleton makes an evolution or two, fires at the Dragoons & obliges them to retire... the Picquets throws themselves into the Park yt was on our left, continues there fire where Stapleton was wounded, & are at last obliged to give themselves up as prisoners of War.'

Consequently when Murray came running back in search of support for the collapsing right wing he found just two battalions still unengaged – the *Royal Ecossois* and Lord Kilmarnock's newly raised Footguards. Both regiments followed him forward, but it was already too late and as the surviving clansmen dissolved into rout the *Royal Ecossois* exchanged token volleys with Campbell's 21st (Scots Fuziliers) and then began to retreat in good order. Sensibly enough they first moved to their right and then fell back along the Culwhiniac Park wall, where they were masked from artillery fire. Unfortunately they had reckoned without the half battalion of Loyalist Highlanders commanded by Captain Colin Campbell of Ballimore.

When Hawley had earlier cleared the parks and led his dragoons out on to the open slope below Culchunaig he left Ballimore's men behind.

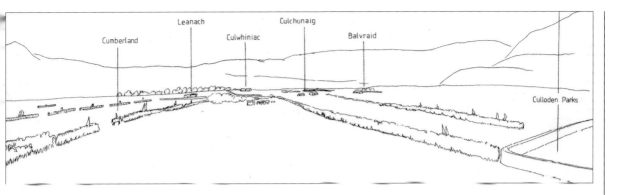

Cumberland Leanach Culwhiniac Culchunaig Balvraid Culloden Parks

This of course was in accordance with the earlier orders that they should avoid contact with rebel units and so prevent the possibility of 'blue on blue' incidents. Nevertheless, since Hawley, intentionally or otherwise, neglected to specifically order Ballimore to retire to the baggage train the gallant captain decided to get in on the fight after all.

Moving up the slope inside the park Ballimore initially opened fire at long range on some of the Jacobites lining the re-entrant near Culchunaig. This firing was of little more than nuisance value, but 'though few were killed by reason of the distance yet many were wounded, especially in the legs and thighs.' Now as the *Royal Ecossois* fell back beside the wall, Ballimore ambushed them, firing a volley into their flank. It is not entirely clear whether he himself was then killed leading a sortie out through the gate, or was moving parallel with the retreating mercenaries and shot as he moved out of cover past it, but at any rate Campbell of Airds sadly reported that; 'It was in passing a slap (opening) in the second Dyke that Ballimore was Shot Dead, and that Achnaba received his wound of which he Dyed next day.' Five other men in Ballimore's company were afterwards returned as dead and three wounded in this firefight – most of them apparently shot through the head.

Brief though the encounter was, it was still sufficient to drive Kilmarnock's men and the *Royal Ecossois* back out on to the moor and, unwittingly, throw them into the path of Hawley's dragoons.

Up until this point Hawley, rather to the frustration of some of his junior officers (including young James Wolfe), had been content to remain passively observing the strong force of Jacobites posted along the crest in front of him. But now, as Wolfe related: 'as soon as the Rebels began to give way and the Fire of the Foot slacken'd, he [Hawley] ordered Genl Bland to charge the rest of them with three squadrons, and Cobham to support him with two'.

This entailed the three squadrons of Kerr's 11th Dragoons moving through the intervals in Cobham's two – who were originally in front – and fight their way across the re-entrant. Happily it was not much of a fight for the Rebels were evidently already beginning to withdraw. Nevertheless Kerr's subsequently reported three men killed, three others wounded and the loss of no fewer than 19 horses, so they must have been in receipt of at least one volley from the rebels, who subsequently got away without further molestation.

Cobham's had a much easier time of it and emerging straight on to the moor they gave some of the rebels a very nasty shock indeed. Not realising that the British cavalry were already roaming about in the

ROYAL ECOSSOIS AT CULLODEN (pages 82–83)

As the Jacobite army crumbled into bloody ruin, one of the few units to cover its retreat was Lord John Drummond's *Royal Eccosois*, a regiment of Scots mercenaries in the French service. In fact at the moment when the Highlanders broke there remained only three regiments still not engaged. Behind the left wing the red-coated Irish Picquets briefly stood against Cumberland's cavalry, while on the right wing were Lord Kilmarnock's newly-raised Footguards and the *Royal Eccosois*. Kilmarnock's men (1) appear to have disintegrated almost immediately, but Drummond's blue-bonneted mercenaries (2) initially retired in good order by alternate wings or battalions (3). Keeping close by the Culwhiniac park walls in order to avoid the fire from the British guns they fought off an ambush by Ballimore's loyalist highlanders, only for about half of them to be surrounded by Hawley's dragoons, who came in on their rear. The rest escaped southwards to Ruthven Barracks with a number of other units and consequently relatively few appeared on the initial lists of prisoners marched into Inverness. At Ruthven however the last remnants of the rebel army were disbanded and as an English volunteer named John Daniel recalled, while most went on the run either for home or to the coast with the hope of finding a boat to France, those officers with French commissions made their way north to surrender. One of the officers who did so was Captain Donald MacDonald (4) of Benbecula. The second son of Ranald MacDonald of Clanranald he had originally joined the French Army in 1742 as a cadet in the Irish regiment Rooth. In 1744 he was transferred as one of the original cadre of the newly formed *Royal Eccosois* and returned with them to Scotland in 1745 as a captain. Despite having been born in Scotland and being the younger brother of young Clanranald, one of the more prominent of the Jacobite leaders, he was sufficiently confident of his status as a French officer to surrender at Inverness after Culloden. His confidence was not misplaced, for although there were sufficient doubts to keep him imprisoned in Edinburgh Castle until October 1748, he was then released with the benefit of a free pardon. However he did not then return to the French service, instead in 1757 he joined a new Highland regiment being raised by Simon Fraser, the erstwhile Master of Lovat, and at Quebec two years later his ability to speak French and his knowledge of French military routines first allowed Wolfe's flotilla of boats to descend the St. Lawrence without being intercepted, and then later on the cliff-top, he bluffed his way into a French picquet post and so secured the head of the vital Foulon road. (Gerry Embleton)

Jacobite rear area, Lord Kilmarnock blithely rode up to Cobham's, mistaking them for the redcoated Fitzjames's Horse, and was lucky not to be summarily shot. The *Royal Ecossois* fared little better for at about this time an English volunteer named John Daniel recalled meeting Lord John Drummond, who 'desired I would come off with him, telling me all was over and showing me his regiment just by him, surrounded'. In actual fact the *Royal Ecossois* may have been retiring by alternate wings, for while part of the regiment certainly surrendered on the field after losing about 50 killed or wounded, their distinctive colours were not taken and a substantial number of men led by a Major Hale succeeded in getting away with the rest of the low-country regiments that had stood above the re-entrant.

Their stand may also have given the Prince himself precious time to escape. When the MacDonalds finally broke he appears to have been rallying Perth's and Glenbuchat's regiments but Sullivan immediately rode to Captain Shea at the head of the Prince's escort squadron and shouted: 'yu see all is going to pot. Yu can be of no great succor, so before a general deroute wch will soon be, Sieze upon the Prince & take him off…'

Shea did his duty and hustled him away safely, accompanied by Perth's and Glenbuchat's men, and as it broke up the rebel army effectively divided itself in two. The Lowland regiments which had been posted above the re-entrant retained some kind of order and retired southwards, crossed the Water of Nairn and eventually made their way to Ruthven Barracks. However, with this particular escape route cut almost at once by the dragoons moving up from the south, the Highland regiments from the front line were forced to take the understandable but fatal course of running straight back down the road to Inverness. It was just the situation which every cavalryman dreams of. Led by Bland, all of the dragoons set off after the fugitives and 'gave Quarter to None but about Fifty French Officers and Soldiers He picked up in his Pursuit'.

Although the vigorous and undoubtedly bloody pursuit was afterwards represented in some quarters as tantamount to a war crime, it was in reality nothing out of the ordinary and indeed the Highlanders themselves had proved equally ruthless when the position was reversed. As James Wolfe, who probably took part in the pursuit himself, remarked: 'The Rebels, besides their natural inclinations, had orders not to give quarter to our men. We had an opportunity of avenging ourselves for that and many other things, and indeed we did not neglect it, as few Highlanders were made prisoners as possible.'

It was impossible of course to compile accurate returns of rebel casualties, but most estimates reckoned that around 1,500 Jacobites were killed or wounded, besides an initial 154 rebel and 222 'French' prisoners taken. However, a further 172 of the Earl of Cromartie's men

William Boyd, Earl of Kilmarnock. Early in the rising he recruited a regiment of 'Horse Grenadiers' in the Falkirk area, but after it had to be dismounted his mother-in-law, Ledy Erroll helped him recruit a regiment of 'Footguards' in Aberdeenshire, which may have been as much as 300 strong at Culloden.

were taken prisoner by Loyalists in a neat little action at Dunrobin on the day before in order to make up the official total of 326 subsequently quoted in Cumberland's despatch. Afterwards allegations were rife that hundreds of rebel wounded were executed out of hand, although the British Army's attitude was summed up by the unnamed officer of the 37th who wrote that: 'Our Regiment had ample revenge for the Loss of our late Colonel, Sir Robert [Munro], and the rest of our Officers, whom the Scoundrels murdered in cold blood, but (as I told Lord Kilmarnock) we had ample Revenge in hors. For I can with great Truth assure you, not one that attack'd us escaped alive, for we gave no Quarters nor would accept of any.'

Nevertheless the total of prisoners rose dramatically over the next few days as wounded men were brought in from the moor. While it was freely admitted that a number of wounded rebels were executed out of hand, these were on the whole isolated incidents carried out by unsupervised parties of the despised 'Vestry men', who had been assigned to battlefield clearance.

As for the British Army, the regimental returns recorded just 50 dead and 259 wounded, although a high proportion of the latter must have actually died. For example only 29 out of the 104 rank and file returned as wounded in Barrell's 4th Foot afterwards survived to claim pensions from Chelsea, and all six of the Royal Artillerymen returned as wounded succumbed to their injuries.

AFTERMATH

All in all, it seems likely that after the preliminary manoeuvring and deployments had been completed the actual battle may have lasted no more than about 20 minutes, but decisive as it was it did not end the campaign. Having beaten the rebels on the moor Cumberland's first priority was to complete his victory by seizing Inverness. Strictly speaking this was accomplished without meeting any resistance, first in a rather disorganised fashion by some of Bland's dragoons and then more formally by a company of Sempill's 25th (Edinburgh) Regiment commanded by Captain Campbell of Ardkinglas.

In the meantime a rather odd incident occurred. As the first of the rebel fugitives came running down the Inverness road they were met by a battalion of Frasers commanded by their chief's son, the Master of Lovat. According to well-established tradition the Master promptly faced his men about and marched them straight back to Inverness with colours still flying and pipes playing. What happened next is a good deal less clear. There are two other traditions concerning the bridge in the town that crosses the river Ness. One, not improbably, relates that the Master of Lovat proposed to hold it until dissuaded by some local worthies, but the other rather more intriguingly describes a skirmish when the bridge was seized by a party of the Argyll Militia who tried to block any Jacobite retreat across it. That there was such a fight is confirmed by James Johnstone, who recalled hearing a short but intense burst of firing from the town just before the dragoons arrived. However, while the presence of the Argylls may reasonably be doubted it is entirely possible that the rather slippery Master of Lovat changed sides and that his men tried to block the bridge against their erstwhile colleagues. This would certainly explain a near miraculous rehabilitation that followed and saw him die a lieutenant-general in the British Army.

Others were less lucky. Having taken possession of the town, released the British prisoners held there and replaced them with Jacobite ones, the Duke of Cumberland paused to take stock, and appears to have made an offer of amnesty to the rebel leaders as well as to their followers. With renewal of the campaign in Flanders imminent he was understandably reluctant to take his army into the hills in pursuit of the rebels, and at first the indications were that he might not have to.

After the battle most of the Highlanders either dispersed or retired straight through Inverness to Fort Augustus, where they were joined by Barisdale's MacDonalds and a small battalion of MacGregors. The Lowland regiments on the other hand moved south, by way of Corrybrough, to what seems to have been a prearranged rendezvous at Ruthven Barracks. Upwards of 1,500 men assembled there but then orders came from the Prince, directing them to 'shift for themselves'. Similar orders must have been sent to the units gathered at Fort Augustus and for all practical purposes the Jacobite Army was disbanded on 18 April. Those officers and men of the

A unique pair of sketches depicting Bagot's Hussars, one of the more effective Jacobite reconnaisance units.

Royal Ecossois and Fitzjames Horse who were confident of being treated as prisoners of war returned to Inverness and surrendered there on 19 April, but everyone else simply made for home, or else tried to escape abroad.

A fair number of the Jacobite leaders trekked across the hills to Loch nan Uamh, where the Prince had landed at the outset of the rising and where two French frigates, the *Mars* and the *Bellona*, arrived on 30 April. Two days later the last real battle of the campaign took place when three Royal Navy sloops, the *Greyhound*, *Baltimore* and *Terror*, appeared at the mouth of the loch, and unintimidated by the size of the French ships launched an immediate attack. The engagement lasted about six hours, before the little sloops drew off to lick their wounds and during that time the Jacobites on shore frantically dodged cannonballs while carrying off the cargo which had been landed on the beach. Much of it of course was military supplies, but in the 18th century this description almost always included large quantities of alcohol – in this case brandy – and old Coll MacDonald of Barisdale also managed to acquire one of the French longboats, as well as at least one cask of gold.

All in all some £35,000 in gold was landed from the ships. Without it Cameron of Locheil and the other surviving clan chiefs might have responded positively to Cumberland's offer of amnesty, but instead buoyed up by this apparent proof that their French allies had not deserted them, they took the fatal decision to fight on. On 8 May at a meeting held at Muirlaggan, near the head of Loch Arkaig, Lochiel, Lochgarry, Clanranald and Barisdale all agreed to call out their men once more and bring them to a rendezvous at Invermallie on 18 May, where they would be joined by the remains of Keppoch's men, and Cluny MacPherson's regiment, which had not been at Culloden.

Predictably it all turned into a complete fiasco. Clanranald failed to turn up, while Lochgarry and Barisdale could only muster 300 men between them and then departed a few hours later in search of food. Only Locheil was left at Achnacarry, with the 300 men remaining of his once strong regiment. He still had some hopes of joining with Cluny, but unbeknown to him the MacPhersons had surrendered to the Earl of Loudoun the day before.

Worse still, Cumberland, his patience exhausted, had moved into the hills. His reluctance is evident from the fact that he waited a whole month at Inverness, but having taken the decision to move he acted quickly and decisively. Fort Augustus was reoccupied on 17 May by three regular battalions – Howard's 3rd, Price's 14th and Cholmondley's 34th Foot – and eight Highland companies.

Incredibly Locheil was unaware of this, which hardly argues much ability to conduct a successful guerrilla campaign. Next morning he learned that a body of Highlanders was approaching and for some reason initially assumed that they were Barisdale's men returning; 'but he was soon undeceived by some out-scouts he had placed at proper distances who told him these men were certainly Loudoun's, for they saw the red crosses in their bonnets'. Recognising that it was all over, Locheil ordered his men to disperse without fighting, but by then it was too late to avert the punitive expeditions into the highlands that began a week later and continued throughout the summer.

The bitter legacy of those punitive expeditions, justified as they were, still lingers on today in the popular imagination, but in the years which followed they proved no hindrance to the recruiting of thousands of

Unidentified colour taken at Culloden; and judging by the prominent display of the 'Stuart Arms', probably belonging to Lord Kilmarnock's Footguards. Another possibility might be Colonel John Roy Stuart's Regiment, but tradition holds that his colours were green and were safely carried away from Culloden.

Unidentified colour taken at Culloden; white with a saltire on a blue canton. A very similar flag appears on the arms of Bannerman of Elsick so this colour may perhaps have been carried by his small regiment. Although there is some evidence that it may have stood on the left of the Jacobite second line, it is perhaps more likely that it had been incorporated in Lord Kilmarnock's Footguards.

Highlanders into the British Army. The process began in the immediate aftermath of the rising when 250 rebel prisoners were drafted into Dalyell's 38th Foot on Antigua in July 1746, 100 more to Trelawney's 63rd on Jamaica and 200 apiece to Shirley's 65th and Pepperell's 66th in North America, while in the following year more went into the Independent Companies raised for Admiral Boscawen's expedition against Pondicherry in India.

In the 1750s however men such as Simon Fraser, the one-time Master of Lovat, persuaded the government to allow them to raise complete Highland regiments, and with them died the old Scots mercenary tradition that sent footloose young men abroad into the Scots Brigade in Holland, or the ranks of the *Royal Ecossois*.

FURTHER READING

Study of the campaign has been bedevilled by continual repetition of a number of fundamental errors of fact – such as the movements of Wolfe's 8th Foot – and an over-reliance on Jacobite memoirs. Whilst honestly told those memoirs are inevitably one-sided and the author's *Like Hungry Wolves* (London 1994) is the first modern study of the battle to combine eyewitness testimony from both sides with a thorough study of contemporary tactics, and above all the ground. Notwithstanding its having been based on an outdated framework, John Prebble's *Culloden* (London 1961) remains a powerful account of what it may have been like to fight at Culloden, although the writer's acceptance of atrocity allegations is altogether too uncritical.

A broader picture of the campaign as a whole, and especially the subsidiary operations in the Highlands and North-East Scotland, is contained in *1745: A Military History of the last Jacobite Rising* (Staplehurst 1996). The best and most detailed extant account of the battle of Falkirk is Geoff Bailey's *Falkirk or Paradise: The battle of Falkirk Muir* (Edinburgh 1996). An important (and interesting) account of naval operations is John S. Gibson's *Ships of the '45* (London 1967), while Frank McLynn's *France and the Jacobite Rising of 1745* (Edinburgh 1981) provides a good view of the campaign from the French perspective – it does however follow the modern Julian calendar throughout which can be a touch confusing since all other accounts give dates in 'old' style.

As to the opposing armies, both are covered in some detail in *Like Hungry Wolves* and *1745*, but the best dedicated study of the Jacobite army remains the introductory volume of Sir Bruce Seton Gordon and Jean Arnot Gordon's *Prisoners of the '45* (3 vols. Scottish History Society 1928–29). For the British Army, John Houlding's *Fit for Service: The Training of the British Army 1715–1795* (Oxford 1981) is essential, while Stuart Reid's *Wolfe: The Career of General James Wolfe from Culloden to Quebec* (Staplehurst 2000) will also be found useful.

For the aftermath of the campaign, J.M. Bumstead's *The People's Clearance: Highland Emigration to British North America 1770–1815* (Edinburgh 1982) provides a useful corrective to the popular views of the breakdown of the clan system.

THE BATTLEFIELD TODAY

Even at the time Culloden was recognised as having been an extremely significant event in Scottish history, and the battlefield has attracted a constant stream of visitors ever since. Unlike all too many British sites it remains largely unspoilt and has much to offer both casual visitors and serious students of military history.

In the 18th century the moor was not covered in heather and shrubs, but was instead a broad area of common grazing land chiefly used by the tenants of the Culloden estate, from which it takes its name to distinguish it from the adjacent and much larger Drummossie Moor. It lies some 5 miles outside Inverness and is best approached along the B9006 road from that city – or directly from the A9 trunk road. There is also an alternative approach available from the A92 Aberdeen–Inverness road. Both routes are well signposted and although most visitors will obviously arrive by car or coach, a bracing walk up the road from Inverness is heartily recommended if time allows – the return journey is downhill. One of the attractions of walking this route is that the same road was

Culchunaig today; the present buildings post-date the battle but occupy the original site and still provide a very useful reference point.

used by Jacobite troops marching to the battlefield – and fleeing it afterwards.

The site itself has a large, well-appointed, visitor centre and car park run by the National Trust for Scotland (NTS), situated at Old Leanach in the area occupied by Sempill's Brigade. The visitor centre offers free admission to a good café, toilets and well-stocked bookshop, while payment of the usual fee secures admission both to a museum and interpretative area, and to the adjacent Old Leanach farmhouse. Once thought to have been standing at the time of the battle, recent research has revealed that the present cottage was actually built during the improvement of the estate in about 1760. It does however stand on the site of the earlier steading and according to tradition an adjacent barn full of Jacobite wounded was burned by Cumberland's troops after the battle. In all likelihood, however, given its position, it was probably used as a British Army field hospital.

The National Trust for Scotland also currently owns about a third of the battlefield. A forestry plantation, which obscured much of the Trust's landholding for many years, has been cleared of trees but despite its best efforts a vigorous secondary growth of shrubs and heather is proving much harder to clear at the time of writing. However, that part of the moor immediately adjacent to the recently reconstructed Leanach and Culwhiniac walls is still used for grazing and gives a pretty good idea of its original character and appearance. Similarly although the old Inverness road that slashed across the moor in 1746 has been

Leanach Cottage; the present building dates from about 1760. An earlier turf-walled house and barn on the same site probably served as a British Army field hospital during the battle.

diverted to carry modern traffic clear of the Trust's land, its original course can still be traced quite easily.

A network of paths and unit markers have been set out but current research indicates that they are wrongly placed and generally set too closely together. There are no doubts however as to the scene of the fiercest fighting which is marked by a large oval cluster of mass graves placed on either side of what was the old road, just south of Leanach. It was here that the Jacobites overran Barrell's 4th Foot, only to be hemmed in and cut down in a murderous cross-fire when 'Daddy' Huske counter-attacked. It is all too easy to stand there now amongst the long low mounds and get a feel for what happened on this spot in April 1746.

Further back still and outside the NTS ownership is an access road running through trees from the Inverness road to the currently disused steading at Culchunaig. This access road effectively marks the original position of the Jacobite front line before Lord George Murray's 'changement'. The present buildings at Culchunaig obviously post-date the battle, but they mark where the right wing began the battle and it is well worth continuing down the track to the B851 road. On the left (north) side of the track are the remains of the original Culwhiniac Park wall, and on the right is the open field, cultivated in 1746 but now used for grazing, where Hawley waited with his cavalry until the battle on the moor had been won. The re-entrant itself is prominent and easily found, but the field is private property and visitors should behave appropriately.

A whole day should be allowed for a comprehensive visit if it is intended to walk out from Inverness, and as most of the moor is still as boggy as it was in 1746; a stout pair of boots is essential if it is intended to stray off the official paths. Otherwise the site *can* be comfortably viewed in a couple of hours, leaving ample time for a subsidiary visit to the magnificent Fort George (1757) at nearby Ardersier. Other local sites worthy of attention include the Civil War battlefield of Auldearn, just outside Nairn, and Ruthven Barracks, overlooking the A9 near Kingussie.

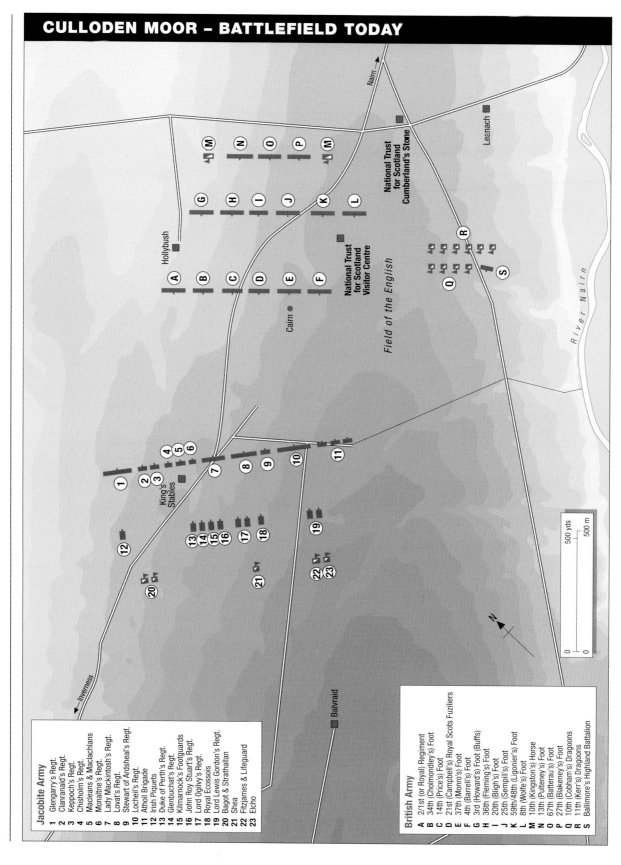

Nairn

Leenach

National Trust
for Scotland
Cumberland's Stone

M N O P M

G H I J K L

R

Hollybush

A B C D E F

National Trust
for Scotland
Visitor Centre

Q S

Field of the English

Cairn

River Nairn

Inverness

King's
Stables

1 2 3 4 5 6 7 8 9 10 11

12

13 14 15 16 17 18 19

20

21 22 23

N

500 yds

500 m

0

0

Balvraid

Jacobite Army

1 Glengarry's Regt.
2 Clanranald's Regt.
3 Keppoch's Regt.
4 Chisholm's Regt.
5 Macleans & Maclachlans
6 Monaltrie's Regt.
7 Lady Mackintosh's Regt.
8 Lovat's Regt.
9 Stewart of Ardsheal's Regt.
10 Lochell's Regt.
11 Atholl Brigade
12 Irish Piquets
13 Duke of Perth's Regt.
14 Glenbuchat's Regt.
15 Kilmarnock's Footguards
16 John Roy Stuart's Regt.
17 Lord Ogilvy's Regt.
18 Royal Ecossois
19 Lord Lewis Gordon's Regt.
20 Bagot & Strathallan
21 Shea
22 Fitzjames & Lifeguard
23 Elcho

British Army

A 2/1st (or Royal) Regiment
B 34th (Cholmondley's) Foot
C 14th (Price's) Foot
D 21st (Campbell's) Royal Scots Fuziliers
E 37th (Monro's) Foot
F 4th (Barrell's) Foot
G 3rd (Howard's) Foot (Buffs)
H 36th (Fleming's) Foot
I 20th (Bligh's) Foot
J 25th (Sempill's) Foot
K 59th/48th (Ligonier's) Foot
L 8th (Wolfe's) Foot
M 10th (Kingston's) Horse
N 13th (Pulteney's) Foot
O 67th (Batterau's) Foot
P 27th (Blakeney's) Foot
Q 10th (Cobham's) Dragoons
R 11th (Kerr's) Dragoons
S Ballimore's Highland Battalion

INDEX

Figures in **bold** refer to illustrations

95

96